John
H...   ...p   616.1

...e

...ases & People

DA...   ISSUED TO

11...   whitney

HEART DISEASE

Other titles in Diseases and People

—Diseases and People—

HEART DISEASE

Philip Johansson

Enslow Publishers, Inc.

40 Industrial Road   PO Box 38
Box 398   Aldershot
Berkeley Heights, NJ 07922   Hants GU12 6BP
USA   UK

http://www.enslow.com

Library of Congress Cataloging-in-Publication Data

Johansson, Philip.
    Heart disease / Philip Johansson.
      p. cm. — (Diseases and people)
    Includes bibliographical references and index.
    Summary: Describes the workings of the heart and the circulatory system and the
array of ailments that can affect them, discussing symptoms, diagnosis, prevention, and
treatment.
    ISBN 0-7660-1051-1
    1. Heart—Diseases—Juvenile literature. [1. Heart—Diseases. 2. Circulatory
system—Diseases.] I. Title. II. Series.
RC673.J64 1998
616.1'2—dc21   97-30804
                                          CIP
                                          AC

Printed in the United States of America

10 9 8 7 6 5 4 3

Illustration Credits: Joan Carey, p. 75; Mayo Foundation, pp. 39, 66, 68, 101;
Philip Johansson, pp. 18, 20, 29, 43, 49, 56, 77, 84, 89; Toshiba America Medical
Systems, Inc., p. 99; *Vermont Sports Today*, pp. 11, 95.

Cover Illustration: Toshiba America Medical Systems, Inc.

Contents

Acknowledgments

The author thanks Dr. Elizabeth Wotton, Susan Kunhardt, John Carey, Joan Carey, and Ro, Zach, Ashley, and Rebekah Corbin-Teich for their helpful comments and unerring eyes. Thanks also to Kate Carter of *Vermont Sports Today*, Dawn Kuehl of Mayo Clinic, and Catherine Eilts of Toshiba America Medical Systems for their expeditious help with photographs.

HEART DISEASE

What is it? A group of related diseases that affect the functioning of the heart and circulatory system.

Who gets it? People of every age can have heart disease, but it becomes more common as people get older. It is also more common in industrialized countries than in developing countries.

How do you get it? Some people acquire heart disease over the course of their lives because of a smoking habit, fatty diet, or lack of exercise. Others are born with a heart defect or with a genetic tendency toward heart disease.

What are the symptoms? There are many possible symptoms, depending on the specific form of heart disease. Patients may experience shortness of breath, dizziness, pains in their chest, nausea, swollen arms and legs, or unusual heartbeats. Many people suffer from heart disease without any perceptible symptoms until they have a heart attack, which can be fatal.

How is it treated? Depending on the severity of the disease, it may respond to changes in lifestyle like dieting, exercising, or quitting smoking. More severe cases may require drug therapy or surgery. Patients with advanced heart disease endure all of the above, and will probably have to for the rest of their lives.

How can it be prevented? Prevention is the best medicine for heart disease, because symptoms often come on so late in its development. Most heart disease can be prevented by having a healthy lifestyle, including exercising, eating right, and not smoking.

1

Not Just for Old Folks

ick was seventeen years old, a senior at an Illinois high school, when the impossible happened. He was an excellent student, but what he liked to do best was play basketball. He played guard for his high school team and was known for his long shots, averaging 20.8 points per game his junior season. Nick was such a valuable player that Northwestern University offered him a basketball scholarship.[1] Everything was going Nick's way when his future crashed down around him.

It happened during a pickup game at the high school with friends. As usual, Nick was playing his best, grabbing a rebound and throwing it the length of the court, when all of a sudden he collapsed in a heap. His heart, which was working hard to circulate oxygen and nutrients to his vital organs and muscles, had stopped. The other players crowded around him.

Nick was unconscious for three long minutes until his father and another adult revived him by using cardiopulmonary resuscitation (CPR). Someone called an ambulance, which rushed the fallen player to the hospital. In the prime of his youth Nick's heart had failed him.[2]

Most young people think that heart disease is something they will not have to worry about until they have gray hair and arthritis. Nick probably thought this way, too, and rightly so. He was physically fit. He ate well and got plenty of exercise. But heart disease is not just for old folks. Many young athletes, such as Nick, who suffer from heart disease have heart defects that have gone unnoticed since birth. Others have weak hearts for a variety of other reasons. Each year ten to twenty-five young American athletes die from heart disease while participating in their sport.[3] Many symptoms are not noticeable except by using advanced medical testing. Even the young and fit are not immune to the possibility of heart disease.

Almost one quarter of all Americans have some type of cardiovascular disease, diseases of the heart or neighboring blood vessels. Cardiovascular disease (CVD) can take the form of high blood pressure, problems with the heart valves or muscle, blockages or narrowing of the arteries, or alterations of the heart's rhythmic pumping. All of these ailments interfere with the vital function of the heart: the circulation of oxygen and nutrients to every part of your body.

More than twenty-five hundred Americans die each day from CVD: that's about one every thirty-four seconds. Almost a fifth of those people are under sixty-five, some of them

Even young people who are in good physical condition should be aware of the dangers of heart disease.

considerably younger.[4] But many more have CVD that may go unnoticed for years. It is certainly something worth finding out about before you have gray hair and arthritis.

Nick was fortunate because he survived his cardiac arrest, but his struggle with heart disease did not end there. His doctors surgically implanted a device in his chest called a defibrillator, designed to jump-start his heart if it ever stopped again. Although he sat out his last basketball season at school, he was well enough to play in several all-star and pickup games the following summer. But when he enrolled at Northwestern University, he discovered he was not playing with its team, the Wildcats, after all. Northwestern gave him his scholarship, true to its word, but the team physician felt that his medical record made him ineligible to play.[5] Nick's safety was apparently more important to NU than his long shots. All Nick wanted to do was play basketball! But this would probably not be the last time heart disease would get in his way.

A Tangle of Diseases

There is an old game called pick up sticks, where players drop a pile of sticks randomly into a heap. Each player takes turns trying to pick out sticks without disturbing others in the pile. It is really a game of the players against the pile, and the pile always wins in the end because players cannot remove all the tangled sticks without a hitch. Learning about cardiovascular disease is exactly the same as playing pick up sticks. It is not a single disease, but a pile of diseases hopelessly tangled together. Any effort to pull out one individual disease, say high blood pressure, cannot help but disturb others in the pile.

Everyone in our modern society has some connection to this tangle. If you do not have cardiovascular disease yourself, then one of your friends might. If no one in your family has cardiovascular disease, their lives may have been changed by someone in their community who does. The tangle threads its way through every aspect of our society. Cardiovascular disease is one of the sadder realities of living in the modern world.

This book will allow you to take apart this tangle of diseases, to dismantle the pile of sticks with a little guidance. You will learn what cardiovascular disease is, where it comes from, and how it is part of our society. Most important, you will find out what efforts you can make to avoid becoming tangled yourself.

2

The Plague of Modern Society

How many young Americans today have had, or have even heard of, smallpox? bubonic plague? polio? Very few! Modern medicine has eliminated the risk of many dangerous diseases that everyone once feared. Such diseases, which once cut down populations throughout human history, are very rare in modern societies. The bubonic plague that wiped out half the population in Europe in the fifth century is unheard of now. But modern medicine has proved no match for the greatest epidemic in modern times: cardiovascular disease. Two out of every five Americans will die from CVD. In fact, more people in the United States die from CVD than from cancer, AIDS, and all other diseases put together![1] How did CVD become the number one killer in America?

Although medical advances wiped out the risk of some diseases, even more disappeared in the twentieth century because of improved hygiene, or general cleanliness. Things we now take for granted, like flush toilets, clean water supplies, and refrigerated food, allow people to live longer, healthier lives without the infectious diseases so common throughout history. In the beginning of this century the average life span was forty-six for white Americans, and thirty-five for nonwhite Americans. Now the average for both is in the mid-seventies, and still rising. Cardiovascular troubles are more common in older people, so living longer lives also increases the possibility of developing CVD.

Ironically, modern medicine and improved living standards may be partially responsible for today's epidemic of CVD. But one of the biggest threats to your cardiovascular health comes from living in a modern industrial society.

The Risks of Modern Living

Besides living longer, there are many other factors that add to the risk of CVD in industrialized societies. Pollution in the air

DECLINE IN DEATH RATE

Between 1982 and 1992, the death rate from cardiovascular disease declined 24.5 percent. At the same time, our population grew, and the percentage of older people grew as well. Because of this, during the same period the actual number of deaths due to CVD declined only 5.5 percent.[2]

and water from factories, cars, and agriculture may make people's hearts more sensitive to disease. Many pollutants such as petroleum products and chlorine promote the formation of "free radicals" in the body, destructive molecules that can damage your body's cells and may lead to CVD as well as to cancer and other diseases.[3] Our bodies must withstand a host of dangerous foreign agents that were unheard of one hundred years ago.

You are what you eat, as the saying goes. If this is true, modern Americans are oil, grease, and fat: hamburgers, French fries, potato chips, ice cream, fried chicken, and scrambled eggs. But many Americans and Europeans ate just as much fat, if not more, one hundred years ago. Many traditional cultures with no history of CVD, such as the Atiu-Mitario of Polynesia, the Greenland Eskimos, and the East African Masai eat high-fat diets of meat and dairy that would make most doctors cry.[4] What is different in our modern society is the nature of the fats we eat, a subject that will be discussed at length in Chapter 7. Modern diets also include more refined foods, like white flour and refined sugar, which lack many natural nutrients that are thought to protect your body from CVD.

The fast-paced high-pressure lifestyles of many Americans may also add to their risk of CVD, and cigarette smoking certainly does. One of the most common behavior patterns in modern society, that of a couch potato who rarely exercises, may also contribute to CVD. Living longer can account for some of the modern CVD epidemic in America, but it cannot

Pollution, noise, unhealthy diets, and high-tension lifestyles are just some of the heart risks of living in the modern world.

account for the increase of this disease in younger people.[5] Cardiovascular disease is a symptom of our modern lifestyles.

History of an Epidemic

Hippocrates, the "father of medicine," recorded the symptoms of a heart attack in ancient Greece as early as the fourth century B.C. He explained that "sharp pains irradiating soon towards the clavicle and back are fatal."[6] But it would still be centuries before CVD became common. It was virtually unknown in Europe and America as late as one hundred years ago, and was absent in traditional societies, like the Eskimo, Pygmy, Masai, and Navajo, into modern times. The first description of a blocked artery in the heart appeared in the medical literature in 1910, when it was still quite uncommon.

By the 1930s and 1940s, the number of deaths due to CVD in the United States was rising at an alarming rate. But one of the most shocking signs of the growing epidemic came in 1953. In the wake of the Korean War, the Pentagon sent doctors into the combat zone with the grizzly task of inspecting dead American soldiers for evidence of how they died. What the doctors did not expect to discover was that three quarters of the victims, all vigorous young men with an average age of twenty-two, had some sign of CVD.[7] This finding was a shock to the medical community, because practically nobody younger than thirty-five ever died of CVD.

By the 1950s, America was in the grip of the cardiovascular disease epidemic, and no one knew why. Some scientists argued that CVD resulted from fat and cholesterol in the diet,

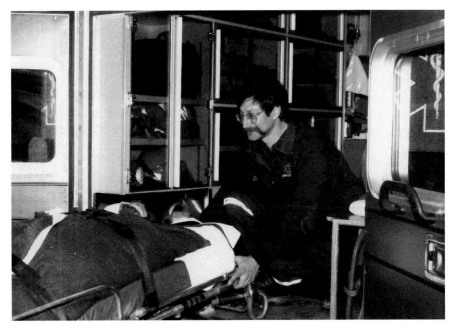

Heart disease is one of the most common causes for ambulance calls.

while others were sure that high blood pressure or cigarette smoking was responsible. Still others felt that several factors contributed to the disease, but exactly which factors were important was open to question. The causes of CVD are still being unraveled by researchers, but some early studies helped to define the debate.

Defining CVD Risk Factors

The first large-scale study to try to find the cause of CVD started in 1948 in Framingham, Massachusetts, a city of twenty-eight thousand, outside Boston. Over five thousand residents between the ages of thirty and sixty-two joined the study, which was conducted by Boston University Medical School. Doctors asked participants about their diets, their lifestyles, and their habits and gave them physical examinations every two years. When signs of CVD showed up in the population, scientists looked for habits that might have led to the disease. The more people with similar habits that showed signs of disease, the surer the scientists could be. Those who are still living continue to participate in the Framingham Study, providing valuable information, and in the 1970s over five thousand more of the participants' children joined the study as well. No other city in the United States has had its health and habits measured for so many years.[8]

Ancel Keys of the University of Minnesota conducted a very different kind of study in 1970. He called the study "Coronary Heart Disease in Seven Countries," and it compared the habits, lifestyles, and occurrence of CVD across seven very different cultures. By comparing Japanese farmers to Finnish factory workers, Italian peasants to United States railroad workers, and Dutch shopkeepers to Yugoslavian food-processing plant workers, Keys was able to find a strong connection between high-fat diets and coronary heart disease. For instance, both were lowest among the Japanese farmers.[9] The Seven Countries study was one of the strongest indications that there was an important connection between diet and CVD. But doctors still debate what that link is.

Other studies focused on the use of drugs to lower the risk of heart disease. The Coronary Primary Prevention Trial in the 1970s measured the effectiveness of the drug cholestyramine in reducing blood cholesterol. But despite the unpleasant side effects endured by the 3,810 subjects, including constipation, gas, heartburn, and bloating, the drug had little result.[10] As was typical until quite recently, this study focused on preventing heart disease in men. CVD is thought of as a men's disease, but recent evidence shows that it is the number one killer of women as well.

The Framingham Study and others like it established that several risk factors play a role in the development of CVD. These include things like age, gender, family history, smoking, high blood pressure, blood-cholesterol levels, and obesity. They will each be dealt with in Chapter 7, which is about preventing CVD in yourself and in others. New risk factors surface every year, and the interactions between factors are still a subject of debate among researchers.

Scientists can all agree that the causes of CVD will challenge them for many years in the future. The death toll from CVD leveled off in the early 1960s and has been on a slow decline since then. But the fact that the average age in the United States continues to increase suggests that CVD will continue to affect more people. Modern medicine will not bring cardiovascular disease to a halt, as it has for other diseases in the past. It will take many changes in our lifestyles, our environment, our diets, and our habits before the plague of modern society becomes part of history.

3

The Heart Is a Lonely Pumper

In 1903, doctors at the University of Chicago performed a historic operation. It was the first heart transplant, and the patient was a dog. Removing the heart from another dog, they transplanted the fresh organ into the neck of the subject, and connected it to an artery. The new heart beat in the dog's neck for several hours until it slowed and finally stopped. For that brief time, the dog had two hearts.[1]

Most people take their heart for granted, even though they only have one. They may have two hands, two legs, two arms, two eyes, and two ears. Unless they have had an operation, they usually have two kidneys, two lungs, two adrenal glands, and two sex organs. They even have two sides of their brain. But they have only one heart, the lonely pumper. Its patient rhythm started when they were three-week-old embryos, and will continue until they die. If the heart stops for more than a few seconds, they will lose consciousness; for more than six to twelve minutes, they will die.

The Vital Role of the Heart

How does this lonely heart keep you alive? Your body requires fuel to work and oxygen to burn that fuel, just as a fire needs to be fanned. Every effort you make requires fuel and oxygen: running after a ball is like a roaring bonfire, but even watching a movie is like a smoldering ember. The heart pumps the oxygen you breathe and the fuel you eat from your lungs and intestines to other parts of your body. These vital ingredients travel in your blood and are distributed by your heart through a complex network of tubes, or blood vessels. The heart and blood vessels make up your cardiovascular system. They work together to deliver fuel and oxygen wherever the fire's burning, from your brain so you can think, to your feet so you can run.

The other role of the cardiovascular system is to make a clean sweep of your body. As your blood returns to the heart it collects waste products from your body, the smoke from the fire, for disposal. Carbon dioxide travels in the blood back to your lungs, where you exhale it. Other wastes flow to your kidneys and liver, which excrete them from your body or safely store them. Without this vital role of the heart and blood vessels, toxic wastes would build up and poison your body.

Structure of the Heart

At the center of this amazing pick-up and delivery system is your heart, the lonely pumper. The heart is a muscle, a hollow mass of muscle cells the size and shape of a person's fist. Weighing in at less than a pound, the heart is a miracle in engineering. Through the simple action of contracting, like your hand squeezing a tennis ball, it is able to circulate more than a gallon of blood through your body every minute of your life. That is over two thousand gallons circulated in a single day or a million barrels of blood in a lifetime: enough to fill more than three supertankers![2]

Put your hand on your chest and you will feel your own lonely pumper. It is in the center of your chest, tucked between your lungs. Two thirds of your heart is to the left of your breastbone, and it tilts slightly so that it is closest to the surface here. It is hard to imagine the gentle thumping under your rib cage being responsible for delivering three supertankers of blood. In order to accomplish this feat, your pint-sized pump must beat around seventy-two times each minute, or over one hundred thousand times a day. How long would your fist last squeezing that tennis ball at that rate? By the time you are seventy years old, your heart will have beaten more than 2.5 billion times. How does this miracle in engineering work?

Inside the heart there are actually two pumps, working side by side. The left pump is bigger, because it has the job of sending blood throughout your whole body. The right pump is smaller and slighter, because it only sends blood as far as the

27

lungs, to pick up more oxygen. A thick muscular wall, or septum, separates the two sides.

Each pump is, in turn, divided into two chambers, an upper atrium and lower ventricle, and pushes the blood through the chambers in two stages. Blood first enters the atrium, a low-pressure pump, then surges into the larger, more powerful ventricle. The relaxed ventricle filling is the first stage, called "diastole." As the ventricle sends the blood on its way with a powerful contraction, it is called "systole." When doctors measure blood pressure, they are looking at the force generated by the heart to pump blood, a good indication of the health of the heart and blood vessels. They measure both your systolic pressure, when the heart is contracting, and your diastolic pressure, when it is relaxed. A normal blood pressure reading is anywhere between 90/60 and 130/90 (systolic/diastolic), though higher readings are considered normal in older people.

The heart is made of a special muscle, the myocardium. This muscle contracts rhythmically when stimulated by an electrical current originating within the heart. Each myocardial cell stores a tiny bit of energy when it is relaxed, like a domino resting in a long line of dominos. When one domino tips, it releases its energy while tipping the next in line, and the next, until all the dominos have fallen. Likewise, when each myocardial cell is stimulated, it contracts and stimulates the next cell in turn.

The electrical current that makes the first heart-muscle cell contract comes from a special group of cells near the top of the

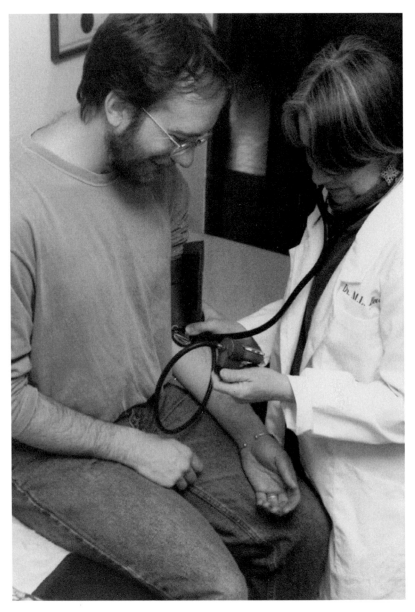

Your blood pressure is generated by the beating of your heart and is a good indicator of heart health.

heart. Doctors call these cells the sinus node, or the heart's "pacemaker." The sinus node not only conducts current like other heart cells, but also independently generates an electrical impulse at least every second. Each impulse from the pacemaker travels through the heart muscle and through other specialized conductor cells to stimulate the contraction of the ventricles. The pacemaker is like the conductor of an orchestra; it sets the rhythm for the beating heart. It is, in turn, controlled by other systems in your body such as your nervous and hormonal systems.[3]

The left and right sides of the heart contract and relax simultaneously. Although the two pumps work together, they send blood in two different directions. Blood from the right atrium and ventricle goes quickly to the lungs where it absorbs oxygen. When it returns to the heart, it goes through the left atrium and ventricle and then on a much longer trip to supply oxygen to the rest of your body. When it returns to your heart again, it has lost all its oxygen, and it goes through the right side to reach the lungs once more. Like an endless highway interchange, all roads lead back to your heart.

If your heart allowed blood to flow freely in either direction inside it, it would be as effective as squeezing a tube of toothpaste with four holes in it. The heart could not be the powerful pumper it is without the strategic placement of four one-way valves. There are valves between the atria and ventricles, and between the ventricles and the vessels leading from them. The familiar "lub-dub" sound that doctors listen for through their stethoscope is the reassuring sound of these

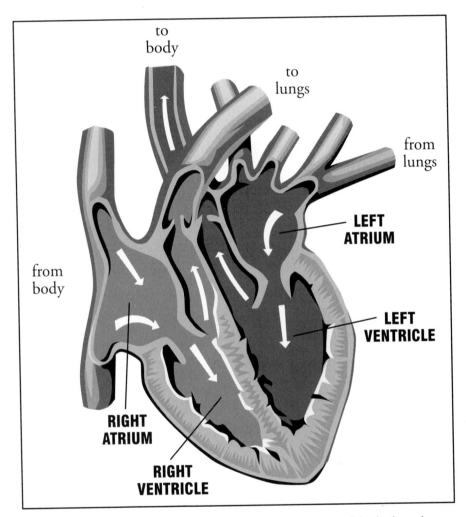

The right side of the heart receives blood from the rest of the body and delivers it to the lungs, while the left side receives oxygenated blood from the lungs and delivers it back to the body.

valves snapping shut. The "lub" is the sound made by the two valves leading into the ventricles, snapping shut as the contraction begins. The shorter "dub" is produced by the other two valves closing as the heart relaxes. Thirty-eight million times a year, these valves keep your blood flowing in the right direction through the heart.[4]

Structure of Blood Vessels

Blood vessels leading from the heart branch like tree roots as they reach your arms, legs, and internal organs. They range in size from the aorta, the main vessel leaving the left ventricle, which has an inside diameter of one and a quarter inches, to capillaries just wide enough to let one microscopic red blood cell pass through them. Vessels leading away from the heart have thick, muscular walls to restrain and absorb the surges of pressure and are called arteries. At the base of the aorta, as it leaves the left ventricle, are two coronary arteries that supply oxygen and nutrients to the heart itself so it can keep up the good work. When arteries branch into smaller vessels, in your heart, in your hand, or in your internal organs, they are called arterioles. These, in turn, branch into smaller and smaller vessels, until they become capillaries.

There are many miles of capillaries wandering through your body, each with sheer walls only one cell thick. Capillaries are so tiny that ten of them together are only as thick as a hair on your head. As the thousands of capillaries pass between the other cells of your body, oxygen and nutrients from your blood trade places with waste products from your cells. Here, in the invisible web of capillaries, the heart's restless pumping finally achieves its goal. Each beat of your heart provides enough oxygen and nutrients to nourish 300 trillion cells.[5]

On the return trip back to the heart, capillaries join to make bigger vessels called venules, which continue joining like tributaries of a river to make even bigger vessels called veins. Veins have thinner, softer walls than arteries because they do not have to withstand the pressure peaks of the pumping heart. Valves along the length of veins help to keep blood moving back toward the heart. The sketchy blue lines on the inside of your arm are veins. Arteries are much deeper inside your body, but you can feel their pulse when you press one against a bone, like in your wrist.

When blood reaches the heart through large main-stem veins, it has come full circle and will be pumped out through an artery to begin cycling again. All this is accomplished by a

YOUR AMAZING HEART

All of your blood vessels laid out end to end would stretch 60,000 miles.

The average heart beats nonstop over 100,000 times in 24 hours.

Your heart pumps 2,000 gallons of blood throughout your body every day.[6]

network of blood vessels more complex and extensive than any road map ever imagined. If all the vessels of your circulatory system—arteries, arterioles, capillaries, venules, and veins—were stretched end to end they would measure about sixty thousand miles![7]

The Cardiovascular System at Work

When you run to chase a ball or to get to class on time, your cardiovascular system jumps to the task. Capillaries in your legs open wider, or dilate, to provide more blood for your working muscles and to divert blood away from other parts of your body. Your heart beats faster to get more oxygen there, sometimes up to two hundred beats per minute, and stretches to push more volume with each pump. If you are running hard, your heart might be putting out blood at a rate three times higher than usual. The quiet lub-dub of your snapping valves becomes a pounding like someone beating on your chest. The coronary arteries supplying the heart itself enlarge to provide ten times as much oxygen to your galloping pumper. Arteries to other parts of your body, including your brain, have to withstand more pounding pressure from the working heart as blood surges to fuel your legs. In terms of a fire, you are a towering inferno.

All of these amazing components of your cardiovascular system contribute to making running, indeed living, possible. But like any miracle in engineering, each of these components has its weakness. Cardiovascular disease occurs when something goes wrong.

4

What Is Heart Disease?

Jim Fixx was a world famous runner who inspired a generation with his book, *The Complete Book of Running,* in 1977. Jim gave Americans back their bodies by bringing cardiovascular fitness to the attention of millions of followers. Shortly after he published his book, the number of runners finishing in United States marathon races topped one hundred thousand, and nine million joggers took to the streets and roads. Jim shocked the nation when he died of a massive heart attack while jogging along a country road in Vermont. He was only fifty-two years old, and apparently as fit as a fiddle.[1]

Jim Fixx's untimely death actually began many years earlier. Jim's father had a heart attack at the age of thirty-six, and died at only forty-three, so he had a strong family history of CVD. Until he was thirty-five, Jim smoked two packs of cigarettes a day. He was fifty pounds overweight and ate a high-fat diet. His life as a magazine editor in Manhattan was stressful, and his only exercise was a "roly-poly game of tennis" on weekends. In a process that started as a child, Jim's arteries became as clogged as a kitchen sink, particularly the coronary arteries that fed his heart. Although no one had ever tested him for heart disease, Jim was a walking, and running, time bomb. In the weeks before his heart attack he even ignored nagging pains in his chest.[2]

Jim's story is a notable one, but he has plenty of company. Over 1.5 million Americans have heart attacks every year, and for one half of them it is their first symptom of CVD. Although some hearts manage to beat for more than one hundred years without rest, there are many problems that can stop or weaken them along the way. CVD represents a group of related disorders that each affects the heart or circulation in its own way. These disorders blur together, so a person with one disorder may be more prone to another. One of the most common is atherosclerosis.

Atherosclerosis

Healthy arteries, the vessels that transport nutrient-rich blood to your body, are muscular and elastic, to allow the pounding pressures of the passing blood. Their interior walls are normally smooth. But many people develop a tough layer of fatty material lining their artery walls, making them narrower and less elastic. The name for this condition is atherosclerosis, which literally means "paste hardening." What starts out as fatty streaks evolves into a complex mixture of cholesterol, calcium, proteins, and cells, called an atherosclerotic plaque. People do not feel a plaque growing in their arteries, and for many this process can begin when they are very young, even infants. Remember the Korean War soldiers in Chapter 2, young men with advanced signs of CVD? More obvious symptoms may show up only in a person's later adult years.

The formation of atherosclerotic plaque is a slow and sneaky process that starts with some damage to the artery wall. The damaged portion is "sticky," and attracts proteins, cholesterol, and fats that form the foundation of the plaque. Blood cells called platelets, which usually aid in blood clotting, get stuck too, and they, in turn, attract muscle cells to grow from the artery wall into the accumulating plaque.[3] The result is like a gooey pizza, with everything, clogging the artery. All this is the blood's normal reaction to any damaged artery, but atherosclerosis occurs when the process spirals out of control.

What damages the artery in the first place, resulting in this gooey mess? Doctors suspect that certain chemicals are responsible for starting the downward spiral. Molecules called free radicals are especially suspicious. Free radicals are produced by our bodies when unhealthy chemicals or other stresses are introduced from the environment, including pollutants, cigarette smoke, pesticides, or even food additives. These renegade molecules cause dangerous chemical chain reactions, wreaking havoc on cells in the arteries and elsewhere.[4]

Your body normally receives more than enough nutrient-rich blood, so artery blockage may be 90 percent before there is any symptom of atherosclerosis. By then, the fatty growth has caused extensive damage to your arteries. Symptoms arise when some part of your body cries out for nutrient-rich blood. Atherosclerosis in the coronary arteries, which supply the heart itself, can result in a heart attack. Blockage of the arteries leading to the brain can cause a stroke. If the blockage is in arteries leading to the retina, blindness can result. If it is in the renal arteries, then kidney failure follows. Atherosclerosis is at the core of many serious cardiovascular disorders, some of which are discussed in the following sections.

Coronary Artery Disease

The coronary arteries that supply the heart with oxygen-rich blood are very vulnerable to atherosclerosis. The heart needs a constant supply of oxygen-rich blood, because it can never take a break, stretch out, or "catch its breath." If the insides of the coronary arteries shrink by 50 to 70 percent of their normal diameter, the reduction of blood flow to the heart can be very serious, even deadly. One tight spot is all it takes. The turbulent blood flow around the plaque makes it a likely spot for a blood clot to form, a fatal combination. Coronary artery disease is responsible for most of the fatalities caused by CVD, causing five hundred thousand deaths a year or one out of every four and a half deaths in America.[5]

When atherosclerosis has blocked a coronary artery so much that the heart's demand for oxygen is not being met, people experience intense pains in their chest, called angina pectoris. Described by victims as "pressure," or "tightness,"

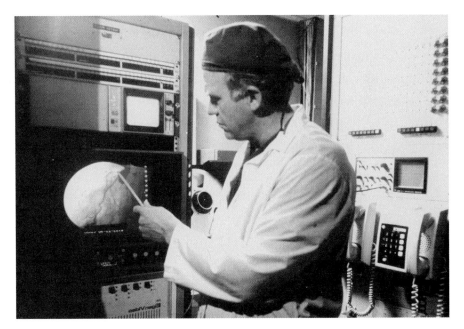

A doctor points to a blocked coronary artery on an angiogram.

angina is the early warning system, the smoke alarm, for coronary artery disease. When the oxygen-starved heart must do extra work, during exercise, emotional upset, cold weather, or after a big meal, the affected muscle activates pain nerve fibers to send a message. Over 2 million people in the United States live with the pain of angina. It is medically treatable, but the recurrent pain is a reminder that their heart is in jeopardy.

A heart attack occurs when atherosclerosis completely blocks one of the coronary arteries, depriving part of the heart of any source of oxygen. Other factors, such as a blood clot or a coronary artery spasm can also contribute to the artery blockage. Within minutes, the part of the heart fed by that artery begins to die. Myocardial infarction, or "heart death," leads to crushing chest pain, described by some victims as though an elephant were sitting on their chest. The pain is more persistent than angina and may include sweating, nausea, fainting, and anxious feelings that the end is near. Even if the heart attack itself is not fatal, it may damage enough of the heart muscle to cause the weakened pump to fail soon after.

In the most lethal cases of heart attack, the lack of oxygen will cause an electrical problem in the heart's conduction system. The heart stops pumping altogether and starts to quiver helplessly like a bag of worms. This is called fibrillation. Unless the heart is pumping again within four minutes, the brain—the most oxygen-hungry organ in the body—begins to die.[6] This kind of "sudden death" heart attack usually leads to death within the first hour, often before the victim reaches the hospital. Although blocked arteries lead to heart attack, fibrillation is usually the final cause of death.

In too many cases the first symptom of coronary artery disease is also the last. After that it is obviously too late to help people with their disease. That is why more and more doctors try to prevent heart attacks by encouraging healthier lifestyles.

Stroke

The brain is an important organ to keep happy. One form of stroke occurs when the blood flow through one of the carotid arteries leading to the brain stops, depriving it of life-supporting oxygen and nutrients. In most cases, this blockage is a blood clot that lodges in an artery narrowed by atherosclerosis. Stroke victims suffer from a loss of many of the vital functions directed by their brains. They experience sudden weakness on one side of their body, loss of speech, loss of vision, dizziness, or sudden falls. Almost one third of the people who have a stroke die from it, usually very quickly.[7]

About one hundred fifty thousand people die each year of stroke. Over three quarters of them are sixty-five or older. Those who survive strokes often suffer from disabilities such as loss of speech or loss of use of their arm or leg. It is the leading cause of disability in the United States. Three million Americans alive today have had strokes in the past, and they are at high risk for having another. Medical treatment has made great strides, but most doctors emphasize preventing strokes in the first place by early treatment of atherosclerosis and another dangerous CVD: hypertension.

Hypertension

If you have ever pumped up a bicycle tire, then you know you have to pump the same number of times to fill up a skinny tire as you do a fat tire. They hold the same amount of air, but the skinny tire is much harder because the air is under higher pressure. The same thing happens when a person's arteries tighten, as in the case of high blood pressure, or hypertension. The same amount of blood must push its way through them, to supply the organs and other parts of the body with oxygen and nutrients, so it flows under much higher pressure.

Unfortunately, understanding the causes of hypertension is much harder than pumping up a bicycle tire. A complex inter-action between hormones, the nervous system, your kidneys, and your heart and blood vessels determines your level of blood pressure, but doctors do not know exactly how. The disease may stem from some of the behavior patterns of modern society, like high stress, smoking cigarettes, drinking too much coffee, and lack of exercise. High salt intake is important in some cases, and some hypertensive patients have a higher salt taste threshold: they have to eat more salt before they taste the saltiness. Obesity can play a role, and for many people, losing just five to ten pounds can normalize their blood pressure.

Some people with hypertension experience headaches, ringing in their ears or bloody noses, but many go years with-out any symptoms. Although perhaps 50 million people have the disease, one third of them has no idea they have it.[8] For this reason, hypertension is called the "silent killer." Many more cases could be revealed if people simply got their blood

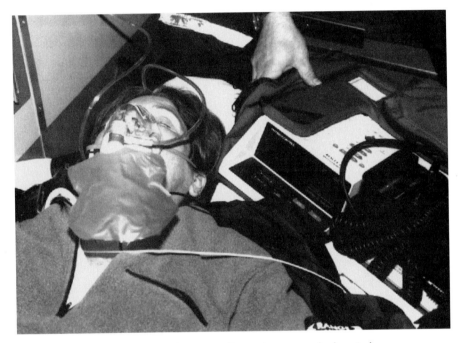

Many heart attack victims die on the way to the hospital.

pressure checked regularly. It would seem that high blood pressure is not a serious problem except for the many dangerous conditions it can lead to.

Blood pushing through arteries at a higher pressure contributes to the buildup of fat or cholesterol on vessel walls, or atherosclerosis. As described earlier, this increases the likelihood of a heart attack if it happens in a coronary artery, or a stroke if it happens in a carotid artery serving the brain. The constant higher pressure within the arteries can also lead to a dangerous weakening of the artery, called an aneurysm. The weak spot can swell up like a balloon, and in some cases it will pop, or rupture—another potentially fatal outcome of hypertension.

Just as it is harder to pump up a skinny tire, the heart must work harder to pump the blood of a person with hypertension. The extra workload makes the heart grow bigger and the heart muscle grow thicker. The added bulk means that the heart requires more oxygen, which is hard for the coronary arteries to provide, and it runs less efficiently. This is why hypertension is one of the leading causes of yet another CVD: heart failure.

Heart Failure

The free market economy operates on a principal of supply and demand, and your heart does, too. A heart attack results from the heart's not being "supplied" enough oxygen and nutrients. Heart failure, on the other hand, comes from too high a "demand" on the heart muscle. For a number of possible reasons, the heart weakens to a point where it can no longer keep blood flowing at the rate demanded by the body. No matter how much it keeps pumping it is losing ground. Blood that should be returning to the heart backs up in other parts of the body instead, causing swelling, tiredness, and fluid in the lungs. Every year fifty thousand Americans die of heart failure, although they respond to treatment in many cases.[9]

Heart failure can come from several causes that weaken the heart. The most common is when a heart attack injures the heart so that it cannot pump efficiently. Just as in the free market, a decrease in supply can result in an increase in demand! Another cause of heart failure is hypertension, when the increased blood pressure strains the heart and makes it enlarged and weakened. High alcohol intake or cigarette smoking can damage the heart muscle, making it weaker, as can certain infections. Heart failure can also result from problems with the heart's valves that make its pumping ineffective.

Valvular Heart Disease

A doctor with a stethoscope can hear heart murmurs when the heart whispers a warning about its valves. Among the familiar lub-dubs of the snapping heart valves, a rushing sound indicates that one or more valves is not working right. Some murmurs are harmless, and 50 percent of all children will have such innocent murmurs at some point in their development. Many pregnant women develop temporary murmurs because of the extra workload on their hearts. But the four one-way valves in your heart enable it to pump efficiently, so any problem with these valves, called valvular heart disease, is a serious concern. Of the four valves, the two on the left side, between the left atrium and ventricle and between the left ventricle and the aorta, are more susceptible to disease.

Valvular heart disease can take several forms. Usually the valves swing open and shut easily, like little one-way doors. But valves can narrow or resist opening all the way as a result of aging or infection. This narrowing is called stenosis. They may also be unable to close all the way, resulting in backflow or regurgitation, following an infection or a heart attack. Valves that just close incorrectly, called prolapsed valves, are usually a congenital or inborn defect. The signs of valvular heart disease can range from no symptoms at all, to fatigue, chest pain, shortness of breath, and heart failure. Approximately 6 percent of the population may have mitral valve prolapse, a defect of the valve leading to the left ventricle, and most of them have no symptoms.[10]

Arrhythmias

Electrical impulses from the sinus node, the pacemaker, cause the heart to beat in a continuous repeating rhythm. However, sometimes part of the orchestra ignores the conductor, leading to abnormalities in the rhythm, or arrhythmias. People with cardiac arrhythmia might feel an irregular beating pattern, called a palpitation, or they might feel nothing. Sometimes people feel palpitations that are merely caused by their own anxiety. Other times palpitations might result from something as simple as drinking too much cola, eating chocolate,

---

PREVALENCE OF CVD

Over 58 million Americans—about 1 in 4—suffer from at least one form of cardiovascular disease. Many people suffer from more than one form, so that people with coronary heart disease may also have high blood pressure or heart failure.[11]

High Blood Pressure: 50,000,000

Coronary Heart Disease: 11,200,00

Stroke: 3,080,000

---

smoking cigarettes, or staying up too late. More consistent arrhythmias can be serious and may be a symptom of other underlying heart disease.

Arrhythmias can occur in the atria or the ventricles of the heart, and range from beating too slow to too fast. The altered heart rate may not meet the body's needs, leading to light-headedness, fainting, and potentially heart failure. When the ventricle is beating too fast, it is called ventricular tachycardia, literally "fast heart." This kind of arrhythmia is serious, because the ventricle is beating too fast to fill up with blood for each pump. Without treatment, ventricular tachycardia can lead to heart failure. Bradycardia, "slow heart," is not usually as serious, and is even common among well-trained athletes. It can also result from the electrical impulses being produced too slowly, say forty to fifty times per minute, or from an interruption in the impulse to the ventricle. Very slow heart rates at fewer than thirty beats per minute can seriously compromise the heart's pumping function.

In the case of fibrillation, the muscle is beating so fast it is just quivering, and pumping basically stops. In atrial fibrillation, the heart's two upper chambers beat at about five hundred times a minute, but the ventricles do not follow suit and only increase to one hundred to one hundred fifty beats per minute. This type of arrhythmia usually stems from other types of CVD and is medically treatable. Ventricular fibrillation is a life-threatening condition and is often associated with a heart attack. Pumping practically stops, and unless normal rhythm is restored within two to five minutes, death results.

Congenital Heart Disease

Flo Hyman was an Olympic volleyball player, the star of the 1984 United States Silver medal-winning team and arguably the best American volleyball player ever. During a game while on tour in Japan, she slumped off the bench and died. At the age of only thirty-one, her aorta developed a tiny balloon-like swelling the size of a dime, called an aneurysm, and popped. She did not suffer from atherosclerosis or hypertension or any of the more common forms of CVD discussed so far. She was marked from birth with a genetic defect called Marfan's syndrome, which affects about thirty thousand people in the United States.[12] Although most cardiovascular diseases are

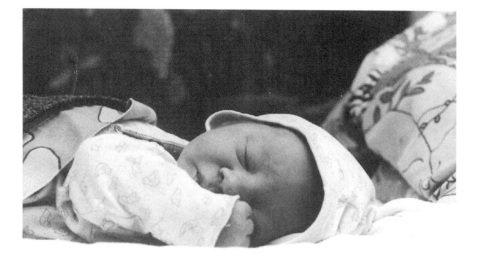

Some forms of heart disease begin before a baby is born.

problems acquired with age and bad habits, there are others that are unavoidable.

Some cardiovascular disorders are present when the heart first forms ten weeks after conception. These are congenital, or "present at birth," heart diseases. The valve defects already mentioned are among the most common congenital defects to affect the heart. For instance, the aortic valve, which usually has three little doors, or cusps, might have only one or two, or up to six, or the cusps can be too small or of unequal sizes. These unusual forms are not necessarily a problem, unless they lead to narrowing or leakage. Their impact may not show up for years, but if untreated they can result in heart failure.

The next most frequent congenital defects, called septal defects, are holes in the walls separating the heart's chambers that allow blood to leak between them. In other cases, the aorta has a crimp as it arches away from the heart. Sometimes the position of the aorta and pulmonary arteries switch places, in a strange twisting of the heart and arteries. In this case some of the blood returning to the heart from the body does not go through the lungs and is not recharged with oxygen. Diagnosis of congenital heart defects requires an analysis of where the blood is being misdirected. For instance, "cyanotic," or blue, babies suffer from not enough blood going to the lungs for oxygen.[13]

About twenty-five thousand babies with heart defects are born every year in the United States.[14] The cause is usually unknown, unless there is evidence of exposure to drugs, German measles, or a chromosome abnormality. Not very long ago, many of these defects would have led to an early death, but new surgical techniques can now treat most of them.

The Tangle of Diseases

The different conditions that are a part of CVD are so interrelated that they are difficult to tease apart. Someone with hypertension is more likely to develop atherosclerosis, and likewise someone with atherosclerosis is prone to hypertension. Hypertension can lead to heart failure, but so can a heart attack or valvular heart disease. Atherosclerosis can be a cause of stroke, but so can hypertension. CVD is a tangle of diseases, but what they all share in common is that they often result from the behavior patterns and diet of modern society.

5

How to Mend a Broken Heart

Over three thousand people in the United States are waiting for a new heart—a heart transplant. Robert Pensack was one of the luckier ones. At the age of forty-two, he got one. A psychiatrist who lives in Colorado, Pensack felt the effects of heart disease at an early age. His mother died at thirty-one, and both Pensack and his brother inherited the genetic disorder that causes a lethal swelling of the heart muscle. Pensack's symptoms started with dizzy spells at the age of seventeen. When he was twenty-one, he suffered a seizure and passed out during a touch-football game. Later, there were fainting spells and attacks of arrhythmia. He had his first artificial pacemaker implanted in his twenties, to keep his heart beating despite its abnormal growth. Then there were numerous drugs. Finally, Pensack's doctors agreed that all the pacemakers and drugs they could give him would not keep him alive.[1]

The only thing that saved Pensack was the untimely death of a twenty-year-old man in a car crash in Texas. The man's heart was rushed to Denver's University Hospital, where Pensack was being operated on in preparation for it. Surgeons removed Pensack's failing heart, and transplanted the Texan's heart in its place. The doctors had trouble starting the heart again, but when it finally began beating, the heart from Texas was pumping Pensack's blood in Colorado. Pensack's health problems are not over. His body has tried to reject the heart, attacking it like a foreign invader, and the drugs to stop this rejection are not pleasant. But when his three-year-old son, Max, listened to his heart with a stethoscope and said "It sounds good, Dad," he knew his trials were worth the trouble.[2]

Not everyone needs a brand new heart. For most cases of CVD, less drastic measures are in order. Depending on the source and severity of the problem, solutions will range from simple lifestyle and diet changes, to drug therapy, to surgical procedures. But before doctors take any action, particularly something potentially dangerous like drugs or surgery, some detective work is in order. It could be a big mistake to treat a patient with valvular disease with drugs for hypertension. Diagnosis is the process of sniffing out the cause of the cardio-vascular problem.

Diagnosing Cardiovascular Disease

Diagnosis of CVD is like putting together a puzzle. A person usually starts a puzzle by finding all the edge pieces first and putting them together, because they are the easiest to find and give the most form to the picture with the least risk. Doctors also use the simplest, least expensive and least risky diagnostic tools to form their initial picture of a patient's CVD. Diagnosis then proceeds in a stepwise progression to more expensive and dangerous tests.

Doctors can draw a very precise picture from the most basic observations: listening to the heart with a stethoscope, measuring blood pressure, feeling pulses of arteries and veins, talking to the patient about his or her health history, or even merely looking at the patient's physical appearance. A patient's gestures, walk, and eyes can tell an observant doctor much about his or her health. Some researchers have even found that a small diagonal crease on the earlobe may be the best predictor of some forms of heart disease![3]

One of the oldest and most reliable diagnostic tests is the electrocardiogram, or ECG for short. By recording the electrical activity of the heart, the ECG can show abnormalities in the heart muscle due to coronary artery blockage, muscle damage, or heart enlargement. Doctors attach ten electrical wires, or leads, to different spots on the patient's chest and arms. Each wire registers a pattern of electrical impulses, representing a different angle on the heart, and displays it on a graph. A small blip represents the electrical signal from the atria, followed by the big blip of the signal

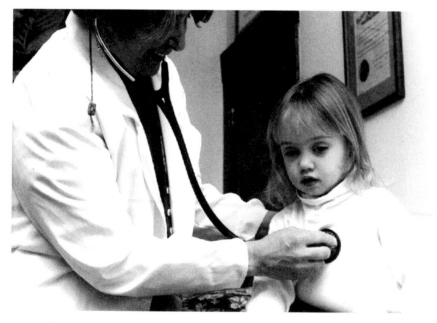

One of the simplest indicators of heart health is the sound of its beating.

from the ventricles. Doctors routinely do ECGs on patients who are even suspected of having CVD, because there is no risk to the patient and a lot of information is obtained.

The trouble with an ECG is that many cases of coronary artery blockage or other heart disease go undetected because the heart is resting when the ECG is taken. An ECG will often appear normal in patients who have symptoms such as angina when they work or exercise. The solution is an exercise stress test, basically an ECG taken while exercising. Doctors attach the patient to the same ECG leads and monitor the heart rate and blood pressure. The patient then walks on a treadmill or rides a stationary bicycle. The exercise brings the patient's heart rate close to its maximum, allowing the detection of narrowed coronary arteries that limit the blood supply to the heart. Exercise stress tests provide a more accurate diagnosis than a resting ECG, and an estimate of what the patient's limits are.

Chest X rays can give additional information about the health of the cardiovascular system. The chest X rays provides information about the size and shape of the heart and is an important part of routine heart evaluation. They are less dangerous than many other diagnostic tests, and they can show heart enlargement and some congenital defects. X rays also clearly differentiate heart problems from lung disease.

If bats had CVD, the echocardiogram would be their choice of diagnostic tool. Doctors use the same sonar used by bats and submarines to look at the heart. They project pulses of ultrasound, with frequencies of millions of cycles per second, through the heart and surrounding organs. The various layers of muscle, bone, and internal organs reflect back the pulses, which the instrument detects and translates into two-dimensional images. The result looks something like a lot of fuzzy curly lines. But a skilled echocardiologist can clearly see the beating heart among the fuzzy curls. Echocardiograms provide valuable information for diagnosing CVD, especially any valve disorders, congenital defects, heart enlargement, or abnormal contraction patterns.

Wouldn't it be helpful if doctors could actually see the blood pumping through the heart? That is the idea behind cardiovascular tests called nuclear scans. Some chemical elements, called radioisotopes, give off a slight amount of radioactivity. In nuclear scans, doctors inject a radioisotope into the blood and then use a special camera to simply photograph the substance as it moves through the heart. Some radioisotopes circulate through the heart chambers, so doctors can see exactly how effective its pumping action is. Others go directly to the heart muscle, so they show areas where the bloodflow to the heart is low due to coronary artery disease. Although the idea of having radioactive material injected into their blood is not appealing to most people, nuclear scans are a relatively safe and useful diagnostic tool.

One of the most important ways to investigate heart disease was invented by a young German doctor in 1929. Werner Forssman imagined that he could insert a tiny tube, called a catheter, into a patient's vein and then slide it along its path until it reached the heart. He envisioned great diagnostic uses for this daring exercise, but his bosses forbade such dangerous research. Forssman had to secretly persuade a nurse to volunteer for the experiment. After she gathered all the necessary sterile instruments he needed, he strapped her to the operating table. Then, despite her protesting, he proceeded to do the operation on himself instead! He made an incision near his elbow and slid the catheter into his own vein and followed it all the way to the interior of his right atrium. He then released the nurse, and they walked down several flights of stairs to the X-ray room to verify the catheter's position![4]

It took another twenty-seven years before the importance of Forssman's brave discovery was fully realized, and doctors did not introduce cardiac catheterization to human patients until the 1970s. Now this relatively safe procedure is one of the most useful diagnostic tools available. Sometimes catheters include blood pressure monitors on the tip, so they can measure the blood flow between chambers of the heart. Most often they inject a special dye into the coronary arteries, allowing an accurate X ray of any blockage or defect, called an angiogram. Since catheterization is an invasive procedure, doctors use it only after all other tests used to assess CVD have indicated its need.

Lifestyle Changes

Once doctors diagnose patients with CVD, they recommend that the patients look at their own lifestyles. Are there things they can change in their day-to-day lives to make their heart healthier? Do they smoke? Do they not exercise? What types of food do they eat? There are many suggestions for lifestyle changes in Chapter 7 (on prevention) that could be a prescription for anyone with CVD. But reversal of heart disease means even more drastic lifestyle changes because the stakes are higher.

For certain types of heart disease, exercise is important. One study showed that only patients who worked hard enough to burn off 2,200 calories a week were successful in rolling back coronary artery blockage.[5] That's only as many calories as a pound of sirloin steak, but it takes six hours of biking to use them up. Patients with coronary disease also have to look at their diets. Most doctors agree that cutting fat intake by at least half is necessary to reverse coronary artery disease. Doctors tell patients with coronary disease to stay away from fried foods, refined foods, and processed oils. Patients are encouraged to eat less meat and fewer dairy products and to eat more vegetables. The benefits for improving your cardiovascular functions are numerous, but exercise or dieting alone will not reverse CVD. This requires a complete program of lifestyle changes, and many people lack the motivation for this.

Another important lifestyle change focuses on emotional health. Dr. Dean Ornish popularized the approach of healing your whole self through his "Opening Your Heart" programs. Based on twenty years of cardiovascular research, Dr. Ornish made the incredible discovery that a complete program of lifestyle changes can reverse some aspects of CVD. Central to his prescribed lifestyle changes are methods for stress management and emotional support. The programs are about "how to enjoy living, not how to avoid dying."[6] Participants feel happier, healthier, and more energetic. Dr. Ornish feels that "We don't have to wait for a new drug, surgical procedure, or technological breakthrough" to roll back heart disease.[7]

Drug Therapy

Not all doctors would agree with Dr. Ornish, and there are plenty of new drugs, surgical procedures, and technological breakthroughs out there to prove it. New drugs, for example, appear every year in the arsenal used against CVD. These drugs can treat the signs and symptoms of heart disease, as well as their cause, but they often have side effects that lifestyle changes do not.

Drugs to correct arrhythmias are among the oldest drugs used for heart disease. In the 1700s, a chemical taken from the foxglove plant, called digitalis, was the first drug of any kind to be scientifically evaluated for its clinical usefulness. Digitalis is still the drug of choice for atrial fibrillation arrhythmia, but in other cases it may not be as helpful. In the meantime, a whole family of antiarrhythmic drugs has grown up around digitalis, to correct every variety of unusual heartbeat. These drugs must be taken in just the right dosage for the desired result, and in many cases unpleasant side effects occur.

Blood thinners and clot dissolvers inhibit the natural clotting process that often contributes to CVD. The original blood thinner, called warfarin, was discovered in moldy hay that caused North Dakota cattle to die from internal bleeding in the 1920s. Because it has the same effect on other animals, people still use it as a rat poison. Warfarin and other blood thinners are useful for patients with certain forms of CVD, but there is always the risk of the same internal bleeding suffered by rats and cattle. A less hazardous and readily available form of blood thinner is aspirin. Aspirin reduces the chances of having a second heart attack or stroke by 25 percent[8] by making blood platelets less "sticky," as described in Chapter 4.

Clot-dissolving drugs are more powerful than blood thinners, and are so effective that they can stop a heart attack in progress by dissolving the clot that is causing it. A patient in the midst of a heart attack has a 20 percent better chance of surviving it with clot dissolvers. But there is a chance of internal bleeding, and patients have to be screened so the clot-dissolving drug can be safely administered.

Doctors recommend cholesterol-lowering drugs only after several months of lifestyle and dietary changes have not affected blood cholesterol levels. These drugs slow the process of plaque growth and stabilize rupture-prone plaques, thus helping reduce mortality from atherosclerosis. Unfortunately, patients who begin taking cholesterol-lowering drugs may have to take them indefinitely, and the drugs may have side effects. These effects include hypertension, heartburn, vomiting, muscle aches, bloating, itching, headaches, dizziness, constipation, and diarrhea.

Many other drugs are commonly used for CVD, including nitrates, alpha-blockers, beta-blockers, calcium channel blockers, and angiotensin-converting enzyme (or ACE) inhibitors.

Each works through a different chemical mechanism to help the ailing heart. Often their effects include relaxing certain blood vessels, slowing the heartbeat, and lowering the blood pressure of the patient. Doctors use these drugs more than any others for the treatment of CVD, often in combination.

Alternative Therapies

Some patients believe that the body is its own best healer and use alternatives to drugs for CVD. These herbs and supplements work to help the health-supporting systems of the body, rather than introduce new substances with potential side effects. Alternative therapies are not generally accepted by the medical community, but they are gaining the attention of some doctors and have been used by alternative practitioners for years. They may be an important part of the solution for some CVD patients.

For instance, a compound called coenzyme Q-10 is an important part of normal cell chemistry, and yet it is deficient in many CVD patients. Taken as a dietary supplement, it can be very beneficial in the treatment of CVD. Dietary supplements can include "antioxidants" that are important for protecting your cells from those rampaging free radicals. These include vitamin E, vitamin C, beta-carotene, selenium, zinc, manganese, and copper.

The berry of the hawthorn tree is one of the most important plant sources for compounds that lower blood pressure, lower cholesterol, and decrease plaque buildup. Mistletoe is useful not only for kissing under at Christmas time, but also as a powerful antihypertensive. Even everyday herbs like garlic and onion have blood pressure- and cholesterol-lowering activity. "Essential fatty acids" are another important tool used by some doctors to balance the impact of dietary fats on CVD, but they will be dealt with more thoroughly in Chapter 7.

Chelation therapy is another alternative to drugs and surgery. Chelation is the process of binding metals to other chemical compounds. Doctors have used chelation therapy for years to remove lead and other metal poisons from patients, but there is some evidence that it can benefit patients with atherosclerosis too.[10] Doctors inject a synthetic amino acid called EDTA into the patient, which binds with copper and iron found in plaques and blocks the production of more free radicals. This procedure is not approved by the government or

THE TASTIEST TREATMENT

Garlic was used by the Egyptians, Babylonians, and Vikings for its medicinal properties. But only recently has its benefit to CVD patients been realized. Although not generally accepted by medical doctors, many alternative practitioners find that garlic has strong cholesterol-lowering activity and lowers blood pressure. It may even prevent the formation or growth of atherosclerotic plaques that threaten to block arteries. Garlic does this by inhibiting the aggregation of blood platelet cells, one of the key ingredients to both plaques and blood clots.[9]

by the American Medical Association, and most doctors frown on it. However, there are enough practitioners out there who believe in the procedure—as many patients receive chelation therapy as receive bypass surgery.

Pacemakers

Imagine an electronic gadget the size of a silver dollar surgically inserted under the skin of your chest, with a wire that gives your heart a jolt of five volts every second. Half a million Americans do not have to imagine it. They depend on artificial pacemakers to keep their hearts beating regularly. Patients receive pacemakers when damage to their heart's own electrical system results in an arrhythmia that cannot be controlled by drugs. The five-volt shock is not strong enough to feel, but their lives depend on it.

There are various designs for pacemakers, but they generally run on lithium batteries that last seven to ten years. Researchers experimented with nuclear-powered batteries in the 1970s, but these proved disappointing. The business end of the pacemaker is a long insulated wire that ends with an uninsulated wire tip. This lead usually threads along a vein into the muscle of the right ventricle.

Balloon Angioplasty

When Werner Forssman gave himself the first cardiac catheter, he never imagined it would work well to blow up tiny balloons. That had to wait until 1977, when doctors performed

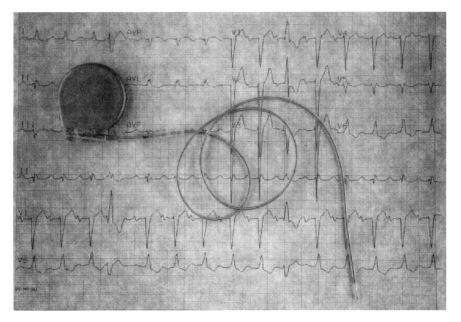

A pacemaker can be inserted to correct irregularities in a patient's heartbeat.

the first balloon angioplasty in Switzerland. They inserted a catheter into a patient's leg artery, then snaked the tube up to his heart and into one of the coronary arteries. The doctors located the plaque blocking the coronary artery by injecting a dye with the catheter. Then they slid a smaller catheter inside the first one and threaded it to the same point. At the end of this tube was a tiny sausage-shaped balloon, which the doctors inflated at the blockage site to compress the plaque against the artery wall. History was made, and the next year doctors did the same procedure in the United States. The following year, they did two thousand. Ten years later there were over two hundred thousand balloon angioplasties performed in the United States.[11]

Balloon angioplasty was a great advance in CVD treatment. Unlike more invasive heart surgery, doctors do not need to knock the patient out entirely; the whole procedure can be done under local anesthesia in the catheterization lab. Recovery is faster and the cost is less than for heart surgery. But angioplasty has its limitations, as when the coronary artery disease is too extensive or is in hard-to-reach arteries. Doctors often use it for very small and accessible plaques in only one of the coronary arteries, but they also apply it for more scattered plaques in some cases. There is always the risk of the coronary artery closing again, requiring the same balloon treatment in a few months. But the use of stents, tiny tubular supports for the collapsing artery, increases the effectiveness of angioplasty.

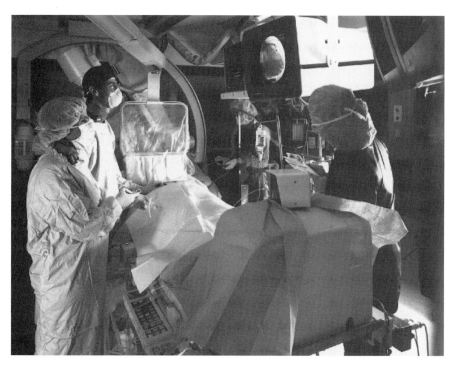

The catheterization lab is the site for angiograms, balloon angioplasties, and other nonsurgical heart procedures.

Heart Surgery

The heart is always beating, keeping its lonely vital rhythm behind the rib cage. Heart surgery was impossible until the invention of the heart-lung machine, which takes over the job of pumping and aerating blood so the heart can take a rest. Developed in 1953, the heart-lung machine was not widely available for heart operations until the 1970s. The machine takes blood from the right atrium and pumps it through a series of thin membranes, which oxygenate the blood just like the lungs, then returns the flow to the aorta. Surgeons clamp the aorta shut tight between the new connection and the heart and inject the heart with a cold solution that stops its beating and preserves its cells for up to six hours. Then the magic of heart surgery can really begin.

Doctors choose to perform heart surgery for a variety of reasons, but usually when there is no other option that would be less risky or less expensive. One tenth of all heart surgery is performed on infants and children, to repair congenital defects like holes in the septum. Doctors perform other heart operations to repair valves that are not working right, or to replace them with artificial valves or valves from a pig's heart. Doctors can also rely on surgery to correct severe arrhythmias, by cutting out unstable areas of muscle that are causing the problem. But the majority of heart operations, over three hundred thousand a year, are for coronary artery disease.[12]

Bypass Surgery

Coronary artery bypass grafts (CABG), or just "bypass" for short, apply the same principle used in traffic detours. Instead of trying to pass traffic through construction areas, workers reroute traffic on another road to avoid the congestion. Bypass operations do the same thing to route blood around coronary arteries blocked by plaques. Surgeons graft a tiny vein from the patient's leg to the blocked artery, on either side of the blockage, which acts as a detour. A patient with two, three, or even four blocked coronary arteries requires a "double," "triple," or "quadruple" bypass operation.

Surgeons performed the first bypass operation in 1967. The procedure became widely available in the 1970s. Now it is one of the most frequently performed of all surgical procedures! Bypass surgery is ideal for high-risk patients with major blockage of all three of the main coronary arteries. Balloon angioplasty is a less traumatic alternative more appropriate for less advanced disease. Both of these procedures restore coronary artery blood flow, but do not reverse the progress of atherosclerosis. Major lifestyle adjustments are still necessary to make that change.

Heart Transplant

Of course, the ultimate heart operation is the heart transplant, such as that experienced by Robert Pensack. Surgeons performed the first heart transplant in 1967, but that patient lived only eighteen days. The third recipient, a retired dentist living in South Africa, lived nineteen months. Breakthroughs in fighting rejection of the new heart, particularly with the drug cyclosporin, have made recent heart transplants even more successful. Eighty-five percent of all heart recipients live more than a year. Sixty-five percent live more than five years.[13] But cyclosporin suppresses the immune system, so the quality of life for heart-transplant patients may be affected by other diseases like pneumonia.

Although over a thousand heart transplants are performed each year, many thousands more patients with severe heart muscle disease or heart failure could benefit. The only thing that is holding them back is the number of donor hearts available and the expense. Robert Pensack was one of the lucky ones. Many heart patients will wait in vain.

6

The Heart of Modern Living

Mr. H thought his way of living was normal.[1] He often lost his temper. He would curse at people that would cut him off in traffic. He would blow up at his wife if she asked about work. He would get so mad at something in the morning paper that he could not finish his breakfast. Mr. H. once counted thirty-three times in one day that he lost his temper, sending his blood pressure through the roof and making his heart race. Mr. H. was an angry and fearful person who felt isolated from others by the stresses in his life. Unfortunately, he was a lot like many other people who live in modern society.

Then Mr. H. had two heart attacks, another symptom of his modern lifestyle. The coronary arteries that feed his heart were over 50 percent blocked. He found it difficult to cross the street without becoming winded. He was on numerous drugs for his illness. All this did was make Mr. H. even angrier. And every time he lost his temper, he only got sicker.[2]

Modern Stress

Traditional risk factors, like age, genetics, cholesterol levels, or smoking, can explain only 50 percent of all CVD cases. Psychological and social factors are also important, although they are harder to measure. Our modern lives are full of stressful situations, from pressures at school or at work to loud noises on subways or in city streets. People experience erratic heart rhythms and other cardiovascular abnormalities while doing something as simple as driving in traffic or speaking in public. Indianapolis 500 racers have higher blood-cholesterol levels after a race, and medical students have higher levels during final exams.[3]

Stress is a normal part of our daily lives. Sometimes even a positive thing can be stressful, such as a new home, a new baby, or a promotion at work. The source of stress is different for everyone, and it does not have to be anything dramatic. For some people, it is breaking up with a boyfriend or girl-friend, for others it is traffic jams or unpleasant people. Stress is not dangerous by itself. It is all in how you react to it. People may be able to avoid CVD by learning to manage their stress.

Thousands of years of evolution have designed our bodies to react to stress by jumping into action. Muscles tighten and digestion stops as blood surges to our muscles. Our breath quickens, our heart rate goes up, and our blood pressure soars. Also, arteries get tighter, blood-cholesterol levels rise, and our

The stresses of school or work can be one of the contributing factors in heart disease.

blood clots more easily. To prehistoric humans, this reaction was essential. They were dealing with dangerous physical stresses like running away from saber-toothed tigers, or lunging at giant woolly mammoths with a spear. Being ready for action probably meant the difference between life and death.

But to modern humans with more ordinary stresses like burnt toast and traffic jams, this response is overkill. Many people are uptight for hours each day, and the physical responses of blood pressure rising and of cholesterol increasing just keep wearing away at their health.[4] The potential impact on cardiovascular health is clear. CVD seems to be as much a part of our modern society as traffic lights and lawyers.

There are several psychological reactions to stress that are unhealthy for the heart. Many people live in the fast lane, with a very competitive approach to work and to life in general. Doctors have connected this kind of type A behavior to CVD for several years. But other emotional factors may be equally important. Many people feel trapped by their situation and its stresses or feel unable to share their burdens. Others feel angry, as if they are alone against the world. People who live alone have more CVD than those who live with someone, or even with a pet or a plant.[5]

Mr. H. was a living example of CVD's role in our society. His everyday stresses ate away at him until he gave in to them. That was the case until he joined Dr. Dean Ornish's "Open Your Heart" program. There are many aspects of the program that helped him, but the most significant change was a new attitude. The support groups in the program broke through

Crowds of people we encounter every day can be stressful for many of us.

Mr. H.'s emotional isolation, allowing him to let go of his fear and rage. The result was that his coronary arteries went from over 50 percent blockage to 13 percent in four years. The only drug that he takes now is one aspirin every other day.[6]

Other Social Factors

Another social factor that contributes to some forms of CVD, particularly coronary disease, is the high-fat American diet. Half of all Americans are overweight, largely because of a love of fatty meats and dairy products.[7] Television advertisements ooze with juicy-looking burgers under a cozy blanket of melted cheese, or gooey hot fudge sundaes smothered with whipped cream. Despite the pressure from meat and dairy industries, the government has acknowledged that our high-fat diet is a serious health hazard facing the country.[8]

Although most people know the health dangers of cigarettes, cigarette advertisements still promote smoking as the "cool" thing to do. Billboards along the road show how smoking cigarettes helps you have more friends or become a cowboy or helicopter pilot. You rarely find magazine articles about the role of smoking in heart disease, because cigarette companies pay a lot of money to advertise in most magazines and newspapers. Even if you do not smoke, chances are you have been in someone's house who smokes, or have stood next to someone in line that does. If so, then you have inhaled secondhand smoke, which is responsible for killing over fifty thousand nonsmokers a year.[10]

THE HIGH-FAT SOCIETY

Around the turn of the century, Sir William Osler observed that the lethal fatty buildup now called atherosclerosis was more common in wealthy people than in poor people. He attributed this difference to the rich meats and other fatty foods that wealthy people could afford to eat. Poor people ate only lowly grains and vegetables and root crops, all very wholesome foods. To Osler, cardiovascular disease was a form of "justice" cast upon the rich in return for their injustices against the poor. The tides have turned today, and the poor are at least as, if not more, likely to eat foods high in saturated fats.[9]

Many cases of CVD may be prevented by changing the habits and behaviors of individuals, the subject of the next chapter. But how can individuals change while their society stays the same? Prevention efforts so far have made a dent in CVD rates, but real change cannot happen without a new social setting where healthy behaviors are the normal thing to do. This new social setting would encourage people to manage their stress better, to eat healthier meals, and to avoid putting unhealthy things like cigarette smoke in their body. But until society can make this positive change, it is up to individuals, like you, to make healthy choices.

7

Habits for a Healthy Heart

reatment of CVD has made great strides in the last thirty years, mainly because of the development of new drugs and breakthroughs in surgical techniques. But too many times the first symptom is disability or death. Because CVD begins so early in life, has few symptoms until it is really serious, and is so difficult to reverse, the most effective treatment is preventing it in the first place. Successful prevention could save millions of dollars in surgery costs and millions of lives.

Risk Factors

The first stage of prevention is identifying people with important risk factors. The Framingham Study, and others like it, identified these risk factors, and the list keeps growing. Three risk factors are beyond our control: age, gender, and heredity. CVD is more common in older people, in men, and in people with a family history of the disease. Other risk factors, like smoking, obesity, high blood pressure, high blood-cholesterol levels, and lack of exercise all come from our modern diets and lifestyles.

But prevention means more than just identifying patients with risk factors. It means taking action to change risky habits, by improving your diet, increasing your exercise, managing your stress, and giving up smoking. These lifestyle changes have proven benefits, and many Americans have taken them to heart. Record numbers are leading healthier lives, and they are partly responsible for the decline in rates of CVD since the 1960s. For many people, these lifestyle changes are very difficult, and often temporary, because they come after a lifetime of bad habits. Healthy habits of diet and exercise are much easier to form when you are young, so the time to start prevention is now.

Family History

Family history of CVD can be an important risk factor for some people. For instance, someone whose father died of a heart attack or stroke before he was sixty has a higher risk of CVD at an early age. Researchers have even identified the genes responsible for some types of CVD. One genetic disorder, found in one out of every five hundred people, results in cholesterol's being removed from the blood too slowly.[1] Another mutation in the gene for a protein called angiotensinogen can result in hypertension.[2] But a family history of CVD is not like a death sentence! One of America's foremost heart doctors says "very few of us, in fact almost none of us, have a family history so strong we can't overcome it."[3] So even for people with CVD in the family, healthy lifestyles will help them avoid the operating table the longest.

Smoking

Everyone knows that cigarettes are bad for you, but few people recognize that smoking leads to more cases of CVD than lung cancer, its more obvious result. Cigarettes are responsible for 21 percent of all deaths from CVD.[4] It is an especially important risk factor for younger people. Nine out of ten young men with severe coronary artery disease are smokers. Smoking is also an important risk factor for women. CVD is the number one killer for women, too, and women who smoke heavily are six times more likely to have a heart attack. The nicotine in cigarette smoke injures artery linings, leading to atherosclerotic plaques, and contributes to blood clotting. Carbon monoxide in the smoke starves the blood of oxygen. Other ingredients make your heart rate rise.

Smoking is the most critical risk factor for CVD that can simply be eliminated. One out of four people smoke. Any smoker can tell you that it is not easy to quit, so the healthiest choice is to never start in the first place. For people who already do have the smoking habit, there are many benefits to quitting and no drawbacks. Within two to three years after stopping smoking, the risk of heart attack drops to the same

One of the easiest heart disease risk factors to avoid is smoking, but quitting once you have started is much harder.

level as that of nonsmokers.[5] Although this drop in risk is not well understood, it gives hope to smokers who want to quit.

Obesity

Obesity is clearly a result of two other factors, diet and lack of exercise. For maximum heart protection, a person's weight should not change appreciably from the age of twenty-one, a pretty tall order for most Americans. Some people are already overweight at the age of twenty-one anyway. People who are overweight are making their heart work harder, and may not give their cardiovascular system the benefits of regular exercise. Their cholesterol levels are higher, as is their blood pressure. Weight distribution is also important. Tummy fat is the most dangerous kind, so even if you are not overweight, fat deposited on your belly is a risk.

Hypertension

Most doctors consider anyone whose blood pressure is consistently higher than 150/90 to have high blood pressure, or hypertension. If untreated, he or she is also four times more prone to severe atherosclerosis. High blood pressure can lead to blood-vessel damage, and to heart failure due to constant overwork. Although the cause of hypertension is not clear, and heredity plays a role, lifestyle changes can help control many contributing factors. Obesity, stress, and lack of exercise all add to the risk of hypertension. Air traffic controllers, who spend their day guiding airplanes full of passengers in and out of busy airports, have four times as much hypertension as most people.[6]

Diet also contributes to hypertension. Some people with the disease have to eat more salt in order to taste it, and their intake of salt may be a risk. More and more people are aware of the dangers of too much salt. But meanwhile the amount of salt in processed food you buy in boxes and bags, known as "hidden salt," has gone up. Controlling hypertension requires carefully reading the ingredients on prepared and snack foods, as well as taking it easy on the saltshaker.

Cholesterol Level

Cholesterol is an essential product of the body used in nerve function, hormone production, and other vital processes. It is present in cell walls, where it protects them from the ravages of free radicals, those rebellious chemicals encountered in Chapter 4. But you can have too much of a good thing. Doctors find a strong association between too much cholesterol in the blood and CVD. When excessive cholesterol flows through arteries and veins, it becomes one of the many ingredients in atherosclerotic plaques.

Doctors determine the amount of cholesterol in your blood with a simple blood test. Levels below 200 milligrams of cholesterol per deciliter of blood are desirable. One out of two adults, and one out of four children, have levels above that.[7] Doctors say that levels between 200 and 239 are borderline, and levels above 240 are high. But having a cholesterol level below 200 is not like having health insurance. Thirty-five percent of the people who have heart attacks have cholesterol levels between 150 and 200.[8] Cholesterol levels are relative, and have to be considered along with other factors. For instance, a seventy-year-old person with no other risk factors could have a level of 260, considered high, with no change in his or her life expectancy.

Cholesterol in blood is like oil in water: they do not mix. So cholesterol in the bloodstream is bound with certain proteins, called lipoproteins, which allow it to mix in. There are many kinds of lipoproteins, but the most important markers for heart disease are high-density lipoproteins (HDL) and low-density lipoproteins (LDL). HDLs are good because they transport cholesterol through the bloodstream to the liver, where it breaks down and leaves the body. LDLs are bad because they bring cholesterol to other tissues, including atherosclerotic plaques. There, LDLs can become part of the chain reactions that make the plaques grow. In addition to testing patients for their total cholesterol, blood tests should also include numbers for HDLs and LDLs. The more HDLs and the fewer LDLs in a person's blood, the better are their chances of avoiding heart disease. Patients are also tested for triglycerides, another form of fatty acids with a strong link to CVD.

Dietary Fats

When patients have a total cholesterol level over 200, the first thing doctors will ask them to do is look at their diet. The role of diet in CVD is very confusing, but most people agree that the amount of cholesterol and fats you eat has some impact on your blood-cholesterol levels. Even a single meal high in fat and cholesterol can make your body release a hormone that causes arteries to tighten and blood to clot. If you eat the standard American diet, one third of the cholesterol in your cells comes from the food you eat.[9] Some foods contain cholesterol, like egg yolk, shrimp, and red meat. But they have a smaller effect on your blood levels than foods with saturated fats, which your body can convert into cholesterol.

Fats are not all bad. They are an important part of your body's metabolism, providing more than two times the calories of an equal amount of protein or carbohydrate. Their concentrated energy is vital for babies and contributes to that satisfying feeling of being "full." Fats help your body absorb essential vitamins like A, D, E, and K. But not all fats are created equal. Some fats are solid at room temperature, because they are "saturated," which means completely filled, with hydrogen atoms. Large amounts of these saturated fats are common in meats, butter, cheese, milk, and coconut and palm oils. Saturated fats make your blood-cholesterol levels go up, and make blood clots more likely. It is no wonder that meat eaters have three times as much CVD as vegetarians.[10]

Unsaturated fats are liquid at room temperature, because they are not saturated with hydrogen atoms. Monounsaturated fats such as olive oil have room for only one hydrogen atom. They also have little effect on blood cholesterol. Polyunsaturated fats, with lots of spaces for hydrogen atoms,

Eating meals high in cholesterol and saturated fats, like most fast food, should be avoided for the health of your heart.

appear to actually reduce the level of total cholesterol in your blood. These fats are common in vegetable oils in varying amounts, with monounsaturated fats being highest in olive and nut oils except for coconut oil.

Part of the benefit of polyunsaturated fats is through the various components, called essential fatty acids (EFAs), they contain. Doctors call these components essential because the body cannot produce them itself. EFAs are important in maintaining the structure of cell membranes. Your body converts some of them to chemical messengers that affect blood pressure and determine the stickiness of platelet cells and, therefore, the degree of blood clotting and plaque formation. You can reach a healthy balance of these hormones by eating a variety of EFAs from vegetable and nut oils. Another valuable EFA found in cold-water fishes may be one of the reasons Eskimos and Japanese, cultures that eat a lot of fish, have such low levels of CVD.

Does the advice on fats end there? Fat chance! Our friends the unsaturated fats can become our worst enemy when they change through processing or heating. Processed oils, like those in margarine, shortening, and many packaged foods, are dangerous because of changes in the structures of their fatty acids. Processing makes them stable at higher temperatures, but also makes them strangers to our digestive system because they are not like natural oils! Processed oils disrupt how the body uses fats, and contributes to clogging your blood vessels. They are no longer beneficial as EFAs and may even become dangerous free radicals themselves! Cooking with oils at high

FAST-FOOD FAT FACTS

Some of the most dangerous foods for your heart are found in fast-food restaurants. If you eat at one, you can make choices that will reduce the impact on your health.[12]

	Saturated Fat	Cholesterol	Total Fat	Calories
Typical Meal:				
Chicken nuggets				
Large French fries				
Vanilla shake				
Total:	*17g*	*94mg*	*45g*	*959*
Lower-Fat Choice:				
Grilled chicken				
1/2 small French fries				
12 oz. cola				
Low-fat frozen yogurt cone				
Total:	*3g*	*62mg*	*16g*	*684*
Typical Meal:				
Cheeseburger				
Large French fries				
12 oz. cola				
Vanilla ice milk cone				
Total:	*16g*	*78mg*	*40g*	*990*
Lower-Fat Choice:				
Hamburger				
1/2 small French fries				
12 oz. cola				
Low-fat frozen yogurt cone				
Total:	*6g*	*38mg*	*19g*	*649*

Better yet, try a salad or a baked potato!

temperature, as when you fry food, can have the same effect, as can letting oils get rancid. Olive oil and other oils high in monounsaturated fats are the most stable and are, therefore, the best for frying.[11]

Before you give up on eating entirely, it is important to remember that some fats are essential to health. Healthful fats are most abundant in unprocessed vegetable and nut oils, whole grains, and other unrefined foods.

Other Dietary Factors

The fats and cholesterol you eat have an important role in preventing CVD, but they are not the only dietary factor. Complete nutritional balance is necessary to make sure all the chemical pathways in your body are in synch, like the parts in a watch. For instance, it is important to eat fiber, like that found in oat bran and beans. Fiber has the critical role of binding the cholesterol you eat as it passes through your intestines, so that it can go right through you. As you might guess, all fiber is not the same. Wheat bran and many other forms of fiber do not dissolve in water, so they cannot serve this useful purpose.

Many people believe that a heart-healthy diet also includes plenty of vitamins and minerals. A five-year study in Canada showed that men who did not take multivitamin supplements were five times more likely to die from a heart attack than those who did take vitamins.[13] Another study showed that a nutritional supplement program was instrumental in stopping the progression of atherosclerosis.[14] Vitamins and minerals serve many purposes, but one of the most important is that they mop up free radicals faster than you can say "pass the butter." Vitamins C, E, and beta-carotene are all capable of this kind of activity. Vitamin B-6, copper, zinc, manganese, and selenium all become part of molecules with the same job. Vitamins and minerals also protect arteries from injury, reduce the stickiness of platelets, and prevent arrhythmia.

Multivitamin supplements are a great precaution, but the best source of these vitamins is a balanced diet, including fruits and vegetables. The key word is balance. Eating potato chips from morning to night is not balanced even if you consider them a vegetable. A balanced diet includes many different sources of protein, carbohydrates, and healthful fats. Protein can come from meat and fish or from beans, nuts, grains, and dairy. Carbohydrates are found in grains, vegetables, and fruits, from pasta to pomegranates. And healthful fats are those found in vegetables and nuts and in the oils made from them. Eating a variety of foods is one of the most important things you can do for your heart.

Stress

We will all encounter stresses in our lives, as described in the last chapter. But an important part of CVD prevention is managing that stress. Proper management can control blood pressure, cholesterol levels, and other physical responses to stress. Stress management means something different for everyone: meditating, stretching out, or even just plain doing nothing. The important thing is that the worries of the day are forgotten. For some people, exercise is the best solution.

Exercise

Many of the symptoms that people considered results of aging are actually the results of disuse. The heart does not get weak and covered with fat because people grow old but because people stop exercising or never exercised in the first place. Sixty percent of American adults are sedentary. They simply do not exercise. Because they prefer to lounge rather than to jog, watch television rather than swim, and sit rather than ski, they have as great a risk of having a heart attack as if they smoked cigarettes.

Exercise improves cardiovascular health by lowering your heart rate and blood pressure, reducing your weight, enlarging your coronary arteries, lowering your response to stress, and magically raising your HDLs, the good lipoproteins in your blood. One study showed that the farther a runner runs, the more his or her HDL levels go up.[15] But you do not have to be a marathon runner to prevent CVD. Any aerobic exercise, such as walking, swimming, bicycling, or skiing, just three days a week, can help prevent the buildup of atherosclerotic plaque, or even reverse it.

Despite the fact that CVD is so common, avoiding it is most often common sense! If you smoke cigarettes; live on a diet of fried foods, snack foods, and ice cream; and your favorite sport is computer games, you are on the wrong track. Some people may have a genetic tendency toward forms of

Exercise is an enjoyable way to lower your risk of heart disease.

CVD, but even people with advanced heart disease can avoid most symptoms if their diets and lifestyles are healthy enough. If you care about preventing CVD in yourself and in others, you can easily show it through your behavior. By not smoking, exercising regularly, managing your stress, and eating a balanced diet, you will help fight the plague of modern society.

8

The Future of Heart Disease

Barney Clark felt like a new man. A few days after his surgery, Clark sat up in his bed and listened to some music. He joked with the nurses. His wife teased him about not loving his family anymore because he no longer had his heart. Clark was the first recipient of a permanent artificial heart, in 1982. Doctors inserted an ingenious device called the Jarvik-7 in place of his ailing heart during a historic operation that took eight hours. His new heart pumped his blood with a flexible diaphragm operated by lines of compressed air.[1]

Clark's story is like a chapter out of a science-fiction book. People have dreamed of artificial organs for years, but Clark was living that dream. This was not the first artificial heart attempted. The very first was in 1969, and was used to sustain a patient for a couple of days while a human donor could be found. But Clark's was the first permanent mechanical replacement, and he lived for 112 days after his transplant. His Jarvik-7 sustained him for over 12 million beats. Clark never left the hospital, and his new life was complicated by valve problems, severe nosebleeds, and the failure of several other organs. He remained cheerful to the end, telling interviewers that "All in all, it's been a pleasure to be able to help people."[2]

The reality of artificial hearts still seems a long way off. Doctors inserted Jarvik-7s into three more patients, with disappointing results. Two patients survived a year, with major complications, and the third lived only ten days. Further development of artificial hearts on a large scale will be very expensive and is not likely to happen in a society so focused on reducing medical costs. Barney Clark's operation alone cost over a quarter of a million dollars. Despite his heroic contribution to the future, we can expect more results from research money spent on prevention and new advances in the diagnoses and surgical treatment of CVD.

In the future, doctors will close in on a better understanding of how CVD develops, how atherosclerotic plaques develop, and why people have heart attacks. They will focus more on prevention and will develop better markers to predict the risk of heart disease. Patients with a family history of CVD will receive genetic tests that will tell them what their risks are.

Diagnosis and testing for CVD will be an area of great growth, as doctors apply the advanced technology now available to more and more cases. New scanning instruments will find their place in the heart doctor's bag of tricks. Positron Emission Tomography (PET) will give vivid colorful images of

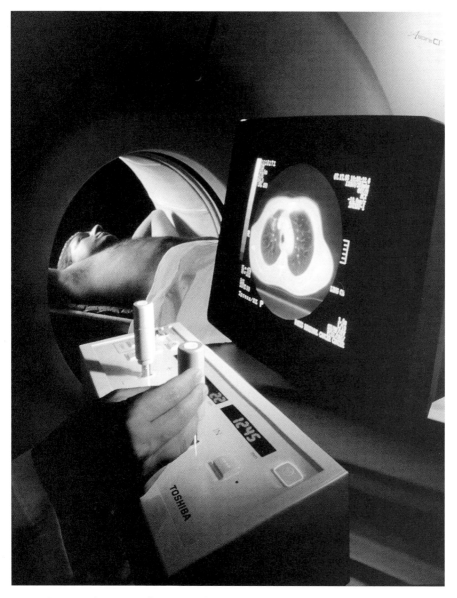

Computed tomography scans will provide more and more accurate images
for diagnosing heart disease.

metabolic activity and blood flow through the heart. Ultrafast Computerized Tomography (CT) will provide 3D images of specific areas, accurately showing diseases of the aorta and other arteries. Magnetic Resonance Imaging (MRI) will allow astounding detail of all the heart's workings, if a reduction in operating costs makes it more accessible.[3] Echocardiograms will incorporate color for more details and accurate identification of tissues, and branch out into 3D renditions. Advances in ultrasound will allow echocardiograms to trace the speed of blood cells moving through the heart.[4]

Treatment for CVD will also reach new heights. New medications are constantly being developed, with hope for breakthroughs in anticholesterol agents and anticoagulants. Improvements in surgical techniques, including anesthesia and the heart-lung machine, will reduce the risks of surgery for those who need it. Two techniques that are now experimental may surpass balloon angioplasty in safely reducing atherosclerotic plaques. Laser surgery will melt plaques away, layer by layer, by inserting a catheter tipped with a laser-heated fiber optic. Doctors will shave off other plaques, using catheters with high-speed cutting drills on the end, rotating one hundred twenty thousand times a minute, a process called atherectomy.[5] Looking farther into the future, advances in genetic engineering may even make it possible to receive a brand new heart that has been "cloned"!

More realistically, the successful transplantation of pig and cow valves will pave the way for transplanting larger parts of the cardiovascular system from animals into humans.

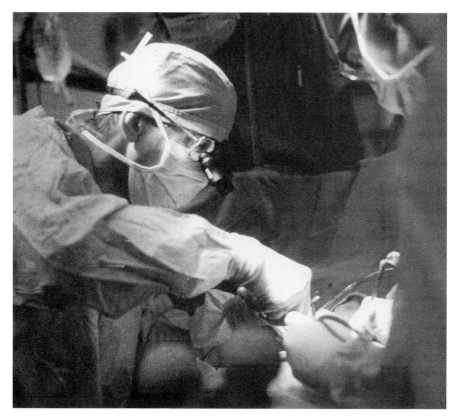

Heart surgery steadily becomes more sophisticated and less risky.

Transplants from animals are called xenografts, literally "foreign" transplants. Doctors hope that the use of animal-heart transplants will overcome the shortage of human donors for heart transplants. A historic example of a xenograft was Baby Fae, an anonymous newborn girl who was dying from a severely malformed heart in 1984. Doctors transplanted a baboon's heart in place of Baby Fae's own, making her the first human to have his or her blood pumped by the heart of another animal. She lived for just a few weeks, but the experiment shed light on the exciting possibility of more successful xenografts in the future.[6]

THE SPEED OF BLOOD

Have you ever noticed when a car goes by how the engine sounds higher before it passes, then lower after it passes? This is called the Doppler effect, and it is due to the frequency of the sound being higher when it is moving toward you. In a sense, the sound waves are being squeezed. In the same way, sound waves are stretched when the car speeds away from you. The same principle is now being applied by echocardiologists to measure the speed of blood cells moving through the heart. High-frequency ultrasound pulses are sent through the body and bounced off of blood cells. The frequency of the reflected wave shows how fast the blood cell was moving! This technique will have exciting applications for CVD diagnosis in the future.[7]

Beyond all the new possibilities in medical technology and breakthroughs in technique, there is the hope that the social and behavioral roots of cardiovascular disease will disappear. This means more than just individuals adjusting their lifestyles, eating better, getting exercise, and stopping smoking, although it will start there. Doctors cannot surgically remove CVD from our society like a failing heart. The change must come from the whole community, including government, industry, and business.

Your role in the future of CVD is critical. It is up to informed individuals like yourself to make healthy choices that will set a good example. Do not smoke, and avoid processed snack food and greasy fast food. Get plenty of exercise, and find ways to manage your stress without letting it grind down your health. The future of your heart is in your hands.

Q & A

Q. Am I too young to be worrying about cardiovascular disease?

A. Most young people do not have to worry about the serious symptoms of CVD, like heart attack, hypertension, or stroke, for a long time. But for many people, the process of CVD starts when they are young. You can do things right now to make it less likely that you will ever suffer from CVD, like not smoking, eating well, and getting exercise.

Q. I thought smoking was just bad for your lungs. Why should I worry about my heart, too?

A. Cigarette smoking actually kills more people through CVD than through lung cancer and other lung disorders. Smoking is the easiest CVD risk factor to eliminate, but it is even easier if you do not start the habit in the first place.

Q. My uncle died of a heart attack. Does that mean I am going to have CVD?

A. No. Like all other risk factors, a family history of CVD merely means you are statistically more likely to contract the disease. The outcome is dependent on all risk factors combined, including diet, exercise, smoking, and stress. The only difference is that family history is one factor you cannot change.

Q. Do I need to stop eating hamburgers to avoid a heart attack?

A. No. A heart-healthy diet can include a limited amount of items with saturated fats like hamburgers, French fries, cheese, and milkshakes. But your diet should also include a lot of fresh fruits and vegetables and whole grains in order to provide your body with the balance of fats and nutrients it needs.

Q. Don't most people survive heart attacks these days, with all the ambulances around?

A. No. Half of all deaths from CVD occur before the patient reaches the hospital. Another 15 percent die once they are in the hospital. The development of CVD is so slow and sneaky that it is a serious situation by the time a symptom arises, often too serious for the most skilled rescue workers.

Q. If I survive a heart attack, what are my chances of making a complete recovery?

A. Two thirds of all heart-attack patients never make a complete recovery. Many of them will have another heart attack within a few years, or experience other symptoms like angina or even a stroke. Others will be disabled by complete heart failure. Your chances are much better if you are under sixty-five years old.

Q. If I was born with a congenital heart defect, would I know it by now?

A. Probably. Most serious congenital defects are discovered soon after birth and dealt with accordingly. But some problems, like minor valve defects or arrhythmias, may not emerge until additional CVD symptoms make them worse.

Q. There are so many different forms of CVD. Why are they all lumped together under one disease?

A. All of the disorders dealt with in this book affect the heart or the blood vessels of the cardiovascular system. They are lumped together because each of them is interdependent upon the others. By avoiding one of them, you will avoid the risk of any number of related disorders. If you eat well, exercise, manage your stress, and avoid smoking, you will be well on your way to complete heart health.

CVD Timeline

4 B.C.—Hippocrates records the symptoms of a heart attack.

1910—The first description of a blocked coronary artery appears in the medical literature.

1918—The only year since 1900 that CVD was not the most common cause of death, because of World War I.

1948—Boston University Medical School begins the Framingham Study, the most comprehensive epidemiological study of CVD.

1951—J. Andre-Thomas devises the heart-lung machine for heart operations.

1953—Pathologists examining casualties of the Korean War discover common signs of atherosclerosis in vigorous young men.

1960—The American Heart Association reports a higher death rate among middle-aged men who smoke cigarettes.

1963—Mortality from coronary artery disease peaks, then declines through the 1970s and 1980s.

1967—Dr. Christiaan N. Barnard performs the first human-heart transplant, in South Africa (patient lives eighteen days); first bypass graft operation, performed in Chicago, Illinois.

1968—First heart transplant performed in the United States.

1970—Nuclear-powered artificial pacemakers are experimentally implanted in three patients; Ancel Keys conducts the study called "Coronary Heart Disease in Seven Countries," drawing attention to the impact of diet on CVD.

1971—A gathering of medical experts called the Task Force on Arteriosclerosis sets an agenda for more research on the causes of CVD.

1977—United States Senate committee issues a report on the dangers of a high-fat diet, called "Dietary Goals for the U.S."; the first balloon angioplasty is performed, in Switzerland.

1982—The first artificial heart, the Jarvik-7, is implanted in Dr. Barney Clark.

1984—An anonymous newborn baby called Baby Fae is the first recipient of the heart of an animal, a baboon.

1986—Mortality from coronary artery disease is 42 percent lower than its peak in 1963.

1987—National Institutes of Health initiates the National Cholesterol Education Program to educate the public about the dangers of high cholesterol levels.

For More Information

American College of Cardiology
Heart House
9111 Old Georgetown Road
Bethesda, MD 20814-1699
(800) 253-4636
http://www.acc.org/

American Heart Association
7272 Greenville Avenue
Dallas, TX 75231-4596
(800) 242-8721
http://www.amhrt.org/

American Red Cross
P.O. Box 37243
Washington, DC 20013
(or call your local chapter)
http://www.redcross.org/

American Society of Hypertension
515 Madison Avenue, Suite 1212
New York, NY 10022
(212) 644-0650
http://www.ash-us.org/

Citizens for Public Action on Blood
Pressure and Cholesterol, Inc.
P.O. Box 30374
Bethesda, MD 20824
(301) 770-1711
http://www.social.com/health/nhic/data/hr0300/hr0345.html

National Heart, Lung and Blood Institute
P.O. Box 30105
Bethesda, MD 20824-0105
(301) 251-1222
http://www.nhlbi.nih.gov/nhlbi/nhlbi.htm

National Stroke Association
96 Inverness Drive East, Suite I
Englewood, CO 80112-5112
(303) 649-9299
http://www.stroke.org/

World Health Organization
525 23rd Street, NW
Washington, DC 20037
(202) 974-3000
http://www.who.ch/

Chapter Notes

Chapter 1. Not Just for Old Folks

1. "The Heart of the Matter," *Sports Illustrated*, November 27, 1995, p. 26.

2. Mike Robinson, "Judge Upholds Hoop Dream of Northwestern Student Whose Heart Stopped," *Indiana Star/News On-Line*, September 9, 1996.

3. Jonas Del Rosario and William Strong, "Sudden Cardiac Death in Young Athletes," *Consultant*, October 1996, p. 2272.

4. "Two Myths About Heart Disease," *Information Please Almanac Annual, 1996*, p. 89.

5. "Heart of the Case," *Sports Illustrated*, September 23, 1996, p. 19.

Chapter 2. The Plague of Modern Society

1. "Heart Disease Leading Killer of Americans," *Information Please Almanac Annual, 1995*, p. 89.

2. "Two Myths About Heart Disease," *Information Please Almanac Annual, 1996*, p. 90.

3. Ralph Golan, *Optimal Wellness* (New York: Ballantine Books, 1995), p. 332.

4. Ibid., p. 47.

5. Bonnie Szumski, ed., *The Health Crisis* (San Diego: Greenhaven Press, 1989), p. 20.

6. Thomas J. Moore, *Heart Failure* (New York: Random House, 1989), p. 18.

7. Ibid., p. 29.

8. Barry L. Zaret, Marvin Moser, and Lawrence S. Cohen, *Yale University School of Medicine Heart Book* (New York: Hearst Books, 1992), p. 24.

9. Moore, p. 75.

10. Ibid., pp. 47–50.

Chapter 3. The Heart Is a Lonely Pumper

1. Barry L. Zaret, Marvin Moser, and Lawrence S. Cohen, *Yale University School of Medicine Heart Book* (New York: Hearst Books, 1992), p. 321.

2. Ibid., p. 4.

3. Jay H. Stein, *Internal Medicine* (Boston: Little, Brown & Co., 1987), p. 303.

4. David E. Larson, *Mayo Clinic Family Health Book* (New York: William Morrow, 1990), p. 784.

5. Zaret, Moser, and Cohen, p. 4.

6. "Heart Health . . . Your Choice," *National Institutes of Health Publication No. 92-3101*, November 1992, p. 3.

7. Zaret, Moser, and Cohen, p. 4.

Chapter 4. What Is Heart Disease?

1. Merrell Noden, "Jim Fixx," *Sports Illustrated*, September 19, 1994, p. 131.

2. Ibid.

3. Michael Murray and Joseph Pizzorno, *Encyclopedia of Natural Medicine* (Rocklin, Calif.: Prima Publishing, 1990), p. 156.

4. Ralph Golan, *Optimal Wellness* (New York: Ballantine Books, 1995), p. 332.

5. Richard Milani and Carl Lavie, "Preventing Progression of Coronary Artery Disease," *Internal Medicine*, April 1996, p. 72.

6. Tony Dajer, "No Surrender," *Discover*, November 1995, p. 50.

7. Barry L. Zaret, Marvin Moser, and Lawrence S. Cohen, *Yale University School of Medicine Heart Book* (New York: Hearst Books, 1992), p. 14.

8. Jay H. Stein, *Internal Medicine* (Boston: Little, Brown & Co., 1987), p. 551.

9. Zaret, Moser, and Cohen, p. 15.

10. Ibid., pp. 15–16.

11. "Two Myths About Heart Disease," *Information Please Almanac Annual, 1996*, pp. 89–90.

12. John Stone, *In the Country of Hearts* (New York: Delacorte Press, 1990), p. 123.

13. Joseph Perloff, *The Clinical Recognition of Congenital Heart Disease* (Philadelphia: W. B. Saunders Co., 1987), p. 5.

14. Zaret, Moser, and Cohen, p. 17.

Chapter 5. How to Mend a Broken Heart

1. Mark Lasswell, "Second Chance," *People Weekly*, March 20, 1995, p. 127.

2. Ibid.

3. Michael Murray and Joseph Pizzorno, *Encyclopedia of Natural Medicine* (Rocklin, Calif.: Prima Publishing, 1990), p. 157.

4. John Stone, *In the Country of Hearts* (New York: Delacorte Press, 1990), p. 150.

5. Marty Munson and Greg Gutfeld, "Another Reversal Route: Can More Exercise Chase Away Heart Disease?" *Prevention*, April 1994, p. 14.

6. Dean Ornish, *Dr. Dean Ornish's Program for Reversing Heart Disease* (New York: Random House, 1990), p. 3.

7. Ibid., p. 2.

8. Richard Milani and Carl Lavie, "Preventing Progression of Coronary Artery Disease," *Internal Medicine*, April 1996, p. 72.

9. John Mann, *Murder, Magic and Medicine* (Oxford: Oxford University Press, 1994), p. 172.

10. Elmer M. Cranton and Arline Brecher, *Bypassing Bypass* (New York: Stein and Day Publishers, 1985), p. 23.

11. Barry L. Zaret, Marvin Moser, and Lawrence S. Cohen, *Yale University School of Medicine Heart Book* (New York: Hearst Books, 1992), p. 306.

12. Ibid., p. 316.

13. Ibid., p. 322.

Chapter 6. The Heart of Modern Living

1. Emrika Padus, "'Open Heart' Without Surgery," *Prevention*, February 1994, p. 60.

2. Ibid.

3. Dean Ornish, *Dr. Dean Ornish's Program for Reversing Heart Disease* (New York: Random House, 1990), p. 13.

4. David Copen and Mark Rubenstein, *Heartplan* (New York: McGraw-Hill Book Co., 1987), p. 32.

5. Ornish, p. 90.

6. Padus, p. 61.

7. Barry L. Zaret, Marvin Moser, and Lawrence S. Cohen, *Yale University School of Medicine Heart Book* (New York: Hearst Books, 1992), p. 51.

8. Patricia Hausman, *Jack Sprat's Legacy: The Science and Politics of Fat and Cholesterol* (New York: Richard Marck Publishers, 1981), p. 36.

9. Ibid., p. 55.

10. G. R. Lesmes and K. H. Donofrio, "Passive Smoking: The Medical and Economic Issues," *American Journal of Medicine*, July 15, 1992, p. 385.

Chapter 7. Habits for a Healthy Heart

1. Thomas J. Moore, *Heart Failure* (New York: Random House, 1989), p. 58.

2. Kathleen Fackelmann, "Teams Hunt for Vascular and Heart Genes," *Science News*, June 11, 1994, p. 374.

3. Kris Napier, "Your Game Plan for Life," *Prevention*, April 1996, p. 101.

4. Richard Milani and Carl Lavie, "Preventing Progression of Coronary Artery Disease," *Internal Medicine*, April 1996, p. 72.

5. Ibid., p. 72.

6. David Copen and Mark Rubenstein, *Heartplan* (New York: McGraw-Hill Book Co., 1987), p. 17.

7. Peter Kwiterovich, *Beyond Cholesterol* (Baltimore: Johns Hopkins University Press, 1989), p. 1.

8. Napier, p. 101.

9. Kwiterovich, p. 9.

10. Michael Murray and Joseph Pizzorno, *Encyclopedia of Natural Medicine* (Rocklin, Calif.: Prima Publishing, 1990), p. 162.

11. Ralph Golan, *Optimal Wellness* (New York: Ballantine Books, 1995), pp. 49–53.

12. "Hearty Habits: Don't Eat Your Heart Out," *National Institutes of Health Publication No. 93-3102*, September 1993, p. 42.

13. Holly McCord, "Low Cost Health Insurance," *Prevention*, March 1995, p. 52.

14. Matthias Rath and Aleksandra Niedzwiecki, "Nutritional Supplement Program Halts Progression of Early Coronary Atherosclerosis Documented by Ultrafast Computed Tomography," *Journal of Applied Nutrition*, March 1996, p. 67.

15. Murray and Pizzorno, p. 168.

Chapter 8. The Future of Heart Disease

1. John Stone, *In the Country of Hearts* (New York: Delacorte Press, 1990), pp. 100–101.

2. Ibid., p. 100.

3. Barry L. Zaret, Marvin Moser, and Lawrence S. Cohen, *Yale University School of Medicine Heart Book* (New York: Hearst Books, 1992), p. 126.

4. Harvey Feigenbaum, *Echocardiography* (Philadelphia: Lea and Febiger, 1986), p. 41.

5. Zaret, Moser, and Cohen, pp. 308–310.

6. David Copen and Mark Rubenstein, *Heartplan* (New York: McGraw-Hill Book Co., 1987), p. 191.

7. Feigenbaum, p. 21.

Glossary

aerobic exercise—Any exercise that challenges the cardiovascular system, such as running, biking, or cross-country skiing.

aneurysm—A swelling and weakening of the artery, often caused by hypertension.

angina pectoris—Tightness in the chest caused by narrowing of the coronary arteries, usually during exercise or emotional distress.

angiogram—Diagnostic test in which a catheter inserted into the coronary arteries injects ink that shows blockages on an X ray.

antioxidants—Naturally occurring compounds that help fight the damaging effects of free radicals.

aorta—The large artery arching from the heart, which distributes fresh blood throughout the body.

arrhythmia—A symptom of heart disease characterized by an unusual or irregular heartbeat, either fast or slow.

arteries—Blood vessels that carry blood away from the heart.

atherosclerosis—A disease characterized by the buildup of fatty material inside the arteries.

atherosclerotic plaque—A combination of cholesterol, calcium, proteins, and cells blocking a portion of an artery.

atrium—The smaller upper chamber found on each side of the heart, which pumps blood into the ventricle.

balloon angioplasty—Procedure that uses a tiny balloon at the tip of a catheter to push aside atherosclerotic plaques that are blocking coronary arteries.

blood clot—Blockage of a blood vessel caused by aggregation of platelets and other blood cells.

bradycardia—Arrhythmia in which the heart beats too slow.

capillaries—Tiny blood vessels where the exchange of nutrients and waste takes place.

cardiac arrest—When a person's heart stops beating, due to interruption of its electrical signals.

cardiopulmonary resuscitation (CPR)—The first-aid method for manually starting a heart that has stopped, involving repeated thrusts to the chest.

cardiovascular disease—A collection of diseases affecting the cardiovascular system, which includes the heart, arteries, veins, and capillaries.

catheterization—Insertion of a small tube, or catheter, into a blood vessel to reach the heart for diagnostic tests and procedures such as balloon angioplasty.

cholesterol—An essential compound used by the body in cell membranes and hormones. Also an indicator used to assess risk of CVD, as it is one ingredient in atherosclerotic plaques.

congenital heart disease—A heart disease that has origins in the development of the cardiovascular system, before someone is born.

coronary arteries—Arteries that branch off from the aorta as it leaves the heart, which supply the heart itself with oxygen and nutrients.

coronary artery bypass graft (CABG)—Surgical procedure in which grafted sections of blood vessel make a detour around blocked segments of coronary artery.

coronary artery disease—Narrowing of the coronary arteries by atherosclerosis, making them vulnerable to blockage by a blood clot or arterial spasm.

diastole—The stage of the heart cycle when the ventricle is relaxed and filling with blood.

echocardiogram—Tool for diagnosing heart disease using high frequency sounds that pass through the body but reflect off the surfaces of organs.

electrocardiogram (ECG)—Diagnostic tool used to monitor the beating of the heart at different angles. Displays waves of electrical activity on a graph, showing weak points.

essential fatty acids (EFAs)—Components of dietary fats that are important parts of cellular function and cannot be produced by the body.

exercise stress test—An electrocardiogram test conducted while the patient is exercising, for more accurate estimate of the heart's limits.

fibrillation—An abnormal heartbeat in which the heart beats so fast it is ineffective. Usually caused by an interruption of the heart's electrical signal, sometimes because of a heart attack.

free radicals—Molecules with an extra electron, known for their destructive activity in living organisms.

HDLs—High-density lipoproteins, responsible for removing cholesterol from the bloodstream.

heart attack—Severe chest pain caused by the complete blockage of one of the coronary arteries, cutting off the blood supply to part of the heart.

heart failure—When the heart muscle is weakened so that it cannot meet the demands of the body.

heart-lung machine—Machine that circulates and oxygenates the blood of a patient during an operation, making heart surgery possible.

heart murmurs—Unusual sounds in addition to the "lub-dub" of the beating heart, indicating a malfunctioning valve.

heart transplant—Surgical procedure in which a patient's failing heart is replaced by the healthy heart of a donor.

hypertension—High blood pressure, a disease characterized by blood pressure over 150/90, which can contribute to risk of atherosclerosis or stroke.

LDLs—Low-density lipoproteins, involved in depositing cholesterol onto atherosclerotic plaques.

lipoprotein—Cholesterol bound with a protein, as it is found in the bloodstream.

monounsaturated fats—Very stable dietary fats found in olive and nut oils, with no negative effects on blood-cholesterol levels.

myocardial infarction—Death of muscle cells caused by a heart attack.

myocardium—Specialized muscle cells that make up the heart.

nuclear scans—Injection of radioisotopes into the bloodstream to monitor where the blood is going or how well the heart is pumping, using a special camera.

pacemaker—See sinus node. Also a device surgically implanted to serve the purpose of a sinus node that is not working correctly.

palpitations—Irregular heartbeat that can be felt by the patient.

platelets—Blood cells that help the blood to clot after an injury. Also an important ingredient in atherosclerotic plaques.

polyunsaturated fats—Dietary fats found in vegetable oils. Some people believe they have a positive effect on blood-cholesterol levels.

saturated fats—Dietary fats that are solid at room temperature and contribute to blood-cholesterol levels.

septum—Muscular wall dividing the two sides of the heart.

sinus node—Specialized cells near the top of the heart that stimulate the heart to contract regularly.

stenosis—When a heart valve is narrowed or resists opening, making it ineffective.

stethoscope—Listening device doctors use to hear the heart and other internal sounds.

stroke—A blockage of the arteries leading to the brain, often caused by atherosclerosis, resulting in damage to some of the brain cells.

sudden death—A cardiac arrest that kills the patient within an hour unless he or she receives medical care first.

systole—The stage of the heart cycle when the ventricles contract, sending high-pressure blood into the arteries.

tachycardia—Arrhythmia in which the heart beats too fast.

valve prolapse—When a heart valve closes incorrectly, usually due to a congenital defect.

valve regurgitation—When a heart valve is unable to close all the way, resulting in backflow and ineffective pumping.

valvular heart disease—When one of the valves within the heart is not working right, resulting in inefficient pumping.

veins—Blood vessels that carry blood from the body back to the heart.

ventricle—The lower chamber found on each side of the heart.

xenograft—Surgical procedure in which an ailing human organ is replaced with an animal-organ transplant.

X rays—Special photograph using very short wavelength light that passes through most bodily organs, useful in diagnosing some forms of heart disease.

Further Reading

Books

Copen, David, and Mark Rubenstein. *Heartplan.* New York: McGraw-Hill Book Co., 1987.

Golan, Ralph. *Optimal Wellness.* New York: Ballantine Books, 1995.

Moore, Thomas J. *Heart Failure.* New York: Random House, 1989.

Ornish, Dean. *Dr. Dean Ornish's Program for Reversing Heart Disease.* New York: Random House, 1990.

Stone, John. *In the Country of Hearts.* New York: Delacorte Press, 1990.

Zaret, Barry L., Marvin Moser, and Lawrence S. Cohen. *Yale University School of Medicine Heart Book.* New York: Hearst Books, 1992.

Articles

Bower, Bruce. "Hopelessness Tied to Heart, Cancer Deaths." *Science News,* April 13, 1996, p. 149.

Bullock, Carole. "Your Heart: A User's Guide." *Current Health 2,* January 1995, pp. 6–12.

Dajer, Tony. "One Step Ahead." *Discover,* April 1994, pp. 94–97.

"No Surrender." *Discover*, November 1995, pp. 50–53.

Fackelmann, Kathleen. "Teams Hunt for Vascular and Heart Genes." *Science News*, June 11, 1994, p. 374.

"Flaws of the Heart." *Science News*, August 3, 1996, p. 76.

"Heart Disease Leading Killer of Americans." *Information Please Almanac Annual*, 1995, p. 89.

"Heart Health . . . Your Choice." *National Institutes of Health Publication No. 92-3101*, November 1992.

Lasswell, Mark. "Second Chance." *People Weekly*, March 20, 1995, pp. 127–128.

McCord, Holly. "Samurai Vegetables." *Prevention*, December 1995, pp. 51–52.

Napier, Kris. "Your Game Plan for Life." *Prevention*, April 1996, pp. 101–111.

Nash, J. Madeleine. "Is a Low-fat Diet Risky?" *Time*, September 5, 1994, p. 62.

Padus, Emrika. "'Open Heart' Without Surgery." *Prevention*, February 1994, pp. 56–64+.

"Two Myths About Heart Disease." *Information Please Almanac Annual, 1996*, pp. 89–90.

Index

cardiovascular system, 26, 34, 57, 83, 100
carotid arteries, 41, 44
chelation therapy, 64–65
chest pain, 36, 38, 46. *See also* angina pectoris.
cholesterol, 19, 22, 37, 44, 82, 86, 87, 88, 91, 92
cholesterol levels, 22, 62, 74, 76, 82, 85, 86–87, 88, 90, 93
cholesterol-lowering drugs, 22, 62
chromosome abnormalities, 50
Clark, Barney, 97–98
clot dissolvers, 61–62
coenzyme Q-10, 63
coffee, 42
computerized tomography (CT), 100
congenital defect, 46, 50, 57, 58, 69
congenital heart disease, 48, 50–51, 58, 69
contraction of heart, 27, 28, 30, 32
copper, 63, 64, 93
coronary arteries, 32, 34, 36, 38, 40, 44, 57, 59, 67, 70, 73, 78, 94
coronary artery blockage, 55, 57, 60
coronary artery bypass grafts (CABG). *See* bypass surgery.
coronary artery disease, 38, 40–41, 58, 60, 67, 69, 83
coronary artery spasm, 40
coronary heart disease, 22, 47, 78
"Coronary Heart Disease in Seven Countries," study, 21–22
cyanotic, 50
cyclosporin, 71

D

death rates, 10, 15, 16, 19, 23, 38, 41, 45, 83

defibrillator, 12
diastole, 28
diet, 10, 17, 19, 21, 22, 23, 36, 51, 54, 60, 78, 82, 85, 86, 87, 88, 90–92, 93, 94, 96, 103
dietary cholesterol, 88, 91
digitalis, 61
disabilities, 41
drugs, 22, 50, 53, 54, 61, 63, 65, 74, 81
drug therapy, 54, 61–63
drug trials, 22

E

echocardiogram, 57–58, 100, 102
electrical current, 28, 40
electrical impulses, 30, 46, 47, 55
electrocardiogram (ECG), 55, 57
emotional health, 60
essential fatty acid, 64, 90
exercise, 10, 17, 36, 40, 42, 57, 59, 60, 82, 85, 94, 96, 103
exercise stress test, 57

F

family history, 22, 35, 82–83, 98
fats, 17, 19, 37, 60, 88, 90, 92, 93
fiber, 92
fibrillation, 40–41, 48
fitness, 35
Fixx, Jim, 35
Forssman, Werner, 58–59, 65
Framingham Study, 21, 22, 81
free radicals, 17, 37, 63, 64, 86, 90, 93

G

garlic, 64
gender, 22, 81
genetic disorders, 53, 82

H

hawthorn berries, 63
health history, 55

S

salt, 42, 86
saturated fats, 79, 88, 91
secondhand smoke, 78
selenium, 63, 93
septal defects, 50
septum, 28, 69
sinus node, 30, 46
smoking, 17, 19, 22, 35, 42, 45, 47, 59, 74, 78, 82, 83, 85, 94, 96, 103
stenosis, 46
stents, 67
stethoscope, 30, 45, 54, 55
stress, 36, 42, 73, 74, 76, 78, 85, 93–94
stress management, 61, 74, 79, 82, 93–94, 96, 103
stroke, 38, 41–42, 44, 47, 51, 62, 82
"sudden death" heart attacks, 40–41
systole, 28

T

triglycerides, 87
type A behavior, 76

U

unsaturated fats, 88, 90

V

valves, 10, 30, 32, 33, 34, 45, 46, 69
valvular heart disease, 45–46, 51, 54, 58
veins, 33, 34, 55, 65, 86
ventricles, 28, 30, 32, 46, 47, 48, 57, 65
ventricular fibrillation, 48
ventricular tachycardia, 47–48
venules, 33, 34
vitamin B-6, 93
vitamin C, 63, 93
vitamin E, 63, 88, 93
vitamins and minerals, 92–93

W

warfarin, 61–62
waste products, 26, 32
women, 22, 83

X

xenografts, 102
X ray, 57, 59

Z

zinc, 63, 93